Just to Follow My Friend

Dear Kay,

Peace and blessings now and always!

Fondly,

Lex 6/10/11

Just to Follow My Friend

Experiencing God's Presence in Everyday Life

Lex Ferrauiola

Tenafly, New Jersey

Fall 2010

Because the Lord is My Shepherd

Because the Lord is my shepherd,
I have ev'ry thing I need.
He lets me rest in the meadow and leads me
to the quiet streams.
He restores my soul and he leads me
in the paths that are right:

Lord, you are my shepherd,
you are my friend.
I want to follow you always,
just to follow my friend.

And when the road leads to darkness,
I shall walk there unafraid.
Even when death is close I have courage,
for your help is there.
You are close beside me with comfort,
you are guiding my way:

Lord, you are my shepherd,
you are my friend.
I want to follow you always,
just to follow my friend.

Your goodness always is with me
and your mercy I know.
Your loving kindness strengthens me always
as I go through life.
I shall dwell in your presence forever,
giving praise to your name:

Lord, you are my shepherd,
you are my friend.
I want to follow you always,
just to follow my friend.

Because the Lord is My Shepherd © 1985, Christopher Walker. Published by OCP 5536 NE Hassalo, Portland, OR 97213.
All rights reserved. Used with permission

For Wanda, my sweetheart and best friend.

You are the sun and the moon and the stars.

and

For Danny, David, Julie and Meg.

You are my joy.

This is a work of love and faith. It is a collection of homilies and reflections since my ordination as a deacon in 1992. I ask God to please bless all those who have helped me on my journey, especially those whom I have hurt along the way.

Table of Contents

Postscript

Monkey Butt

If God really loves us so much why does he allow bad things to happen?

*

I work at Hackensack University Medical Center. At least once each day I ride the elevator in The Tomorrows Children Building. Frequently I share that elevator with young children who are very sick. A few weeks ago I got into the elevator with a young boy, about five years old, and his mother. He was in a motorized wheelchair and appeared to be paralyzed from the neck down — a condition that I assumed had been present from birth. He was unable to speak but could mouthed words that his mom could understand. I was overcome by a feeling of pity for him and his mother; and in my head I started asking a recurring question, "Why God? Why do you let such suffering exist?"

I was distracted from my thoughts by the laughter of the boy's mother. She giggled to her son, "No, you're a monkey butt!" His eyes were bright with laughter as he mouthed the words back to her, "No, you're a monkey butt!" The playful bantering between this mother and child, who obviously loved each other very much, kept up as she wheeled him off the elevator and to whatever life-sustaining treatment he was getting that day.

As I stood alone in the elevator I realized that I had been in the presence of God. God was very much there in the flow of love that went between that mother and child. No matter how much pain and anguish lived in that mother's heart, no matter how debilitated that little boy was, their hearts were totally open to each other, open wide enough to allow themselves to share the gift of laughter and silliness. God was present in the center of the cross shared by that mother and child, just as surely as he is present in the center of the cross that hangs behind me over our parish altar. Our loving God is with us in the midst of all the bad things, all the suffering we experience.

And in witnessing that scene and experiencing that presence of God between mother and child, I can almost understand why God permits suffering.

The bad things that happen and the suffering that exists in life are locked in a moment in time. But God, as well as each one of our immortal souls, is timeless; yet God is with us here in time, holding our hand through the suffering. Some day, when we are free of the limits of our human existence, all the pain and suffering will somehow make sense.

If we could see eternity and the timeless love that awaits us with God, the sufferings that we witness and endure here in life might more easily be understood. God is so good to us that he shows us his face in the suffering. All we have to do is look; all we have to do is listen. God is present in the simplicity of the wind. God is present even in the silliness and the laughter of a word like 'monkey butt'.

September 2000
Ordinary Time

Martha and Mary

Luke 10: 38 – 42

Now as they were traveling along, (Jesus) entered a village; and a woman named Martha welcomed him into her home. She had a sister called Mary, who was seated at the Lord's feet, listening to his word. But Martha was distracted with all her preparations; and she came up to him and said, "Lord, do you not care that my sister has left me to do all the serving alone? Then tell her to help me." But the Lord answered and said to her, "Martha, Martha, you are worried and bothered about so many things; but only one thing is necessary, for Mary has chosen the good part, which shall not be taken away from her."

*

Life is a journey from Martha to Mary. A journey from being scattered to being whole; from being worried and bothered about many things, to resting peacefully in the presence of God. But success on this journey doesn't depend on reaching a destination; on waking up one morning and finally having become Mary. Success happens when we realize that God loves us unconditionally whether we happen to be Martha or Mary.

Before we were born and even before we were conceived, each one of us was a little soul known and loved by God and destined to live with him for all eternity. Like a mother loves her child, God loves us. When we are happy and at peace, God sings for us; and when we are hurt and broken, God weeps.

But life is hard, things get scary and sometimes we forget — or maybe we never really had a chance to understand — that God loves us forever. And like Martha we become worried and bothered about many things.

Then along comes Jesus into our life, just like he came to Martha and Mary's house for dinner 2,000 years ago. He comes to us through the Eucharist; he comes to us through other people, people who love us. And Jesus speaks to the Martha within us — that part of our mind that is worried and bothered.

"Be still for a while," Jesus tells us. "Let me hold you. Rest your troubled head upon my chest and let my love and my peace envelop you. There is need for only one thing: reach beyond that part of you that is Martha, that part that has been hurt and broken, and find that part of you that is Mary, that part at your center, and know that I love you and am with you for always."

Life is a journey from Martha to Mary but let us not forget that both of these holy women are saints. We may want to transform ourselves from the anxiety-ridden Martha with her Type A personality into the peaceful, centered, Zen-like Mary. But let us be mindful that there is holiness at both ends of this spectrum; and that as human beings we are never *either* Martha or Mary, but *both* of these holy women at the same time. And let us never ever forget that God loves us unconditionally at any given moment whether we happen to be Mary or Martha.

July 2007
Ordinary Time

Just Practicing

One of the many, many nice things about being a deacon is that we can be married and have a family. Anyone who knows me knows how incredibly fortunate and blessed I am to be married to Wanda, my high school sweetheart and best friend for more than 42 years. And they know how blessed we both have been with our four children Danny, David, Julie and Meg. All four are leading productive lives and involved with good and interesting work.

Our older daughter Julie is a third year medical student doing her clinical rotation at a Level 1 trauma center in Brooklyn. Julie recently shared a powerful experience with us. Wanda and I saw its relevance to our faith, and Wanda encouraged me to share it with the parish.

Julie was on call in the ER when an elderly lady was brought in by ambulance from a nursing home. The lady's name was Linda and she was having difficulty breathing. But in addition to her physical problem, Linda's chart showed a diagnosis of schizophrenia. This poor woman's internal world was a terrifying place.

Julie was assigned to Linda to do a work-up that included drawing blood and listening to her heart rate. Linda was fearful of the needle but Julie's calming presence reassured her. With one gentle stick, Julie was able to draw the necessary blood without causing Linda any pain. Linda felt safe with my daughter and asked her name. "Julie," she gently answered.

In listening to Linda's heartbeat, Julie discovered something irregular. The intern who was supervising her confirmed the irregularity and asked Julie to sit by Linda for the duration of her on call shift, and to watch her heart rhythms on the bedside monitor. As she sat down in front of the monitor, Julie gently held Linda's hand. She told Linda that she would be right there just in case she needed her for anything. Linda lay back and was calm.

Less than two minutes had gone by when Linda became very agitated and called out, "Julie."

"Yes, Linda. I'm right here. What do you need?"

"Just practicing." Linda said and lay back peacefully.

Another two minutes went by, "Julie."

"Yes, Linda."

"Just practicing."

And another:

"Julie."

"Yes, Linda."

"Just practicing."

Her interior world being filled with terror, Linda needed to constantly call out to reassure herself that Julie was there. This cycle of calling out and reassurance went on for hours, until Linda was moved from the chaos of the ER and admitted to a room on the elder care unit.

So, how is this relevant to our faith?

Life is a gift and it is beautiful; but the world outside, and inside our head, can at times be painful and frightening. And we live each day with the existential knowledge that our time on earth is limited. But God is always by our side. He will never abandon us. And when our time on earth is through, he will be there to take away our fear, to embrace and welcome us home.

We believe this with faith and someday we will experience it with certainty. But in the meantime we, like Linda, practice to reassure ourselves that he is there; we practice by calling to God in prayer.

And God answers in the darkness, "I am here, my child, I am with you." That answer comes to us in the depths of our hearts, in the love and compassion we receive from others, in the grace of the sacraments; and it comes to us in those unexplained meaningful coincidences that God uses to tell us he's there. God always answers — we just have to be listening.

There have been times in my life when I was scared and felt lost in the universe; times when my back was to the wall and there was no way out. But I called out in the darkness and God always answered and made a window in that wall and pulled me through.

God has been there in the darkness for all of us or we wouldn't be here in this church today. Let us go through this day, this year and the rest of our lives at peace knowing that God is always by our side; and let us keep practicing by calling out to God in prayer. God always answers. It may not be the answer we expect, but God always answers — we just have to be listening.

November 2009
Ordinary Time

All Creation Rightly Gives You Thanks and Praise

Just about every single morning there are some special words from one of our Eucharistic prayers here at Mass that go running through my mind:

"Father, you are holy indeed, and all creation rightly gives you thanks and praise."

Each morning I am blessed to be in the middle of God's creation, and to see and hear that thanks and praise — and I am filled with awe and wonder.

*

The first thing I do when I open my eyes each morning is to thank God for bringing me to another day. The second thing I do is to tell my wife Wanda how much I love her. And the third thing I do is to take my little beagle Katie out on the front lawn for her early morning walk.

Katie is three years old and only 13 pounds. She was a gift from God to us — a loving, gentle spirit. Katie is helping me to move away from my obsessive-compulsive, Type A, workaholic habits, and to be more present to God and to his gifts of creation.

As I circle around the front lawn with Katie, I can hear the birds singing and the owls hooting. I can hear the woodpeckers busily at work. And for those few moments, I feel that I am in God's presence; and I am overwhelmed with a sense of thankfulness and praise for his creation.

While the rest of my day may be tangled in email and meetings; while I spend all too many hours seeing life through the possessive eyes of my ego; those five minutes on the front lawn with Katie open my heart and my soul to God.

And I am filled with a sense of wonder for all God's creation: for Katie herself; for the birds, for the trees; for oceans and sunsets and flowers; for the gift of life and for the unconditional love and forgiveness that can exist between and among human beings.

Life is a gift but it isn't easy. There is joy, but also times of pain and suffering. We all cope with stress, uncertainty and anxiety. But God is always walking beside us, holding our hand — telling us that in the end, it will all be okay.

He sends us this message in the simple gifts of his creation: in the birds, in the owls; in the love we share with others; and even in the loving eyes of a little beagle.

"Father, you are holy indeed, and all creation rightly gives you thanks and praise."

Today is Pentecost, the birthday of the Church. Let us be mindful that all creation is God's Church.

May 2010
Pentecost

Transformation

Acts 2: 1 – 2, 4

> *When the day of Pentecost had come, they were all together in one place. And suddenly there came from heaven a noise like a violent rushing wind, and it filled the whole house where they were sitting. . . And they were all filled with the Holy Spirit.*

*

On that day in Jerusalem on the Jewish feast of Pentecost, the Holy Spirit offered grace and the Apostles said, 'Yes.' Out of that 'yes' the Church was born. And from that point forward the Gospel, the good news that God loves each one of us unconditionally and that death is not the end, spread to every corner of the world in every age — even here to Tenafly.

But for the fifty days leading up to that day, the Apostles, those special friends of Jesus, were dealing with issues of loss, abandonment, grief and self-doubt. They were broken people. They had spent three joyful years with this wonderful man, this miracle worker — who had made each one of them feel as if he or she was the most loved person in the world. And then suddenly, one evening after a lovely dinner, it all ended. Just like that — he was taken away from them and killed; and their hearts were broken in a million little pieces. After the Resurrection they experienced scattered moments of confused elation, but on Ascension Thursday they felt that Jesus had left them forever. So, on that day in Jerusalem on the feast of Pentecost, the Apostles, those special friends of Jesus, were about to give up.

Loss. Abandonment. Grief. Self-doubt. How many of us can relate to that? A parent, a child, a friend, a lover ripped from our lives in an instant. But on that day, that Pentecost, their brokenness was healed. By saying, 'yes' to the Holy Spirit stirring within them, the Apostles were empowered to pick themselves up off the ground. And as a result we are here together in this church 2,000 years later.

We, like the Apostles, are friends of Jesus or we wouldn't be here at Mass. And like the Apostles, we are human beings who during our lifetime must deal with issues of loss, abandonment, grief and self-doubt. We must cope with sickness, death, disillusionment, war, violence and all the uncertainty that surrounds us. But when we meet

Jesus here in Holy Communion, he makes each one of us feel like the most loved person in the world. And as we accept the Eucharist and say, 'Amen' we are really saying, 'yes' to God's grace just like the Apostles did on the day in Jerusalem.

And little by little, day by day, that grace transforms us; and through us the world. It enables us to bring God's Presence into all the circles of our lives: to our families and friends; to the workplace and the classroom; the streets, the highway; the subway, the supermarket, the gym and every place we go.

That grace enables all of us: young and old, male and female, sick and well, married and single, wealthy and homeless, to be instruments of God's peace and love in our troubled world. It enables us to do for future generations what the Apostles did for us.

Today, when the time for Communion comes around, and we are all here together in this one place, if we listen with our hearts as we say our 'Amen', we just might hear the sound of a strong driving wind rushing through our souls. And as we are filled with the Holy Spirit, we, like the Apostles, will be transformed — once again.

June 2006
The Feast of Pentecost

Been to Cana

John 2: 1 – 3, 5 - 11

On the third day there was a wedding in Cana of Galilee, and the mother of Jesus was there; and both Jesus and his disciples were invited to the wedding. When the wine ran out, the mother of Jesus said to him, "They have no wine." . . . His mother said to the servants, "Whatever he says to you, do it." Now there were six stone waterpots set there for the Jewish custom of purification . . . Jesus said to them, "Fill the waterpots with water." So they filled them up to the brim. And he said to them, "Draw some out now and take it to the headwaiter." So they took it to him. When the headwaiter tasted the water which had become wine . . . (he) called the bridegroom, and said to him, "Every man serves the good wine first, and when the people have drunk freely, then he serves the poorer wine; but you have kept the good wine until now." This beginning of his signs Jesus did in Cana of Galilee.

*

Once we've been to Cana, once we've tasted the wine, once we've danced with Jesus, we are never the same again.

There's a wonderful sequence of scenes in Martin Scorcese's film, *The Last Temptation of Christ*. It's the wedding feast at Cana. The head waiter is pointing to the jars, shaking his head at Jesus, and insisting that it's only water. Jesus is smiling and telling him to go and taste it. The waiter finally does and yells over to Jesus, "You're right! It is wine!" Jesus raises his cup and playfully salutes the waiter. In the next scene Jesus is dancing joyfully with the other guests. He is singing and laughing and clapping his hands in the air.

This is the Jesus that I know: a Jesus who is not only with us in our pain and sorrow, but who longs to celebrate each moment of our life with us; who dances with us joyfully and playfully; a Jesus who dances with me — the real me that exists now; not with some idealized me-that-I-should-be, but with me with all my blemishes and imperfections; all my failures and my shame. All he asks of me is that I step into the dance.

Once we step into the dance with Jesus, we are never the same again. Dancing with Jesus changes us forever; it transforms us — sort of like changing water into wine. It doesn't matter to Jesus how well we dance, or if we keep stepping on his toes. He's just happy that we've come to the dance; that we keep trying; that we never give up no matter how many times we fall flat on our backs.

I recently read a short story that speaks about this dance in a very moving way. It is by the Japanese Catholic novelist Shusaku Endo. The story is entitled *The Final Martyrs* and it is set in 17th Century Japan during the persecution of Japanese Christians. The Shogun had declared it a capital offense for a Japanese to practice Christianity.

At first hundreds of people were crucified, burned at the stake, broiled on wooden gridirons or thrown alive into sulfur pits. As the persecution wore on and countless Japanese martyrs held to their faith, the government became more and more enraged and sadistic. It tried to make Christians deny their faith by the cruelest of tortures, and those who renounced Jesus publicly were allowed to go free.

Endo's story is about a group of young adult Christian men who have known each other since childhood. They belong to a village that has secretly practiced Christianity for more than 100 years. One member of the group is named Kisuke. As a child he was big, awkward and accident prone. Being ridiculed often, Kisuke reached adulthood with no self-esteem. As they grew up secretly practicing their faith, the other young men often predicted that if they were ever caught by the government and tortured, Kisuke would quickly renounce his faith and betray Jesus.

The government learns about the village from an informer and it is raided and burnt to the ground. Kisuke and his friends are arrested and confined to a tiny cell to await torture. His friends remain steadfast in their faith and urge Kisuke to pray to Jesus and Mary for strength. But listening to the screams of those being tortured becomes too much for Kisuke. Before his turn comes, he cries to the guards that he is ready to renounce his faith. He leaves the cell in shame never able to look back upon his friends. The other young men are tortured brutally but no one renounces his faith.

For the next two years they are moved around Japan from prison to prison. One by one they begin to die until only two remain. After witnessing so much suffering, their faith has weakened and they are close to despair. And then one day they see a tall awkward figure being led to their cell — it is Kisuke.

After he is shoved into their cell by the guards, his friends ask him how he ended up being brought back for torture after having renounced his faith. Kisuke tells them how he wandered around Japan for two years filled with shame for betraying Jesus. Until one night he could no longer bear it. He stood alone weeping on a desolate beach preparing to end his life. He cried out to the ocean: "Oh, if only I had been born a different person. If only I could have been strong and brave like my friends instead of the worthless coward that I am."

From behind him, Kisuke heard a whispering voice. It was the voice of Jesus: "It's alright, Kisuke. I understand. Just go back to be with the others. Even if the fear and the torture are too much for you to bear and you have to betray me again, it's alright. Just go back to be with the others."

And Kisuke did go back. His friends' faith was renewed by Kisuke's story along with their love for him. As his turn comes to be led to torture, his friends tell him, "It's alright, Kisuke. Even if you have to betray him again, the Lord Jesus is happy. He is happy that you just came back."

There have been many times in my life when I felt like Kisuke standing on that beach. When I looked at my life and reflected on the times that I have betrayed Jesus; the times I have failed to love others; to be present to the people that God has entrusted to my care. But it is at those painful times of self-revelation that I can hear Jesus whispering to me, asking me to dance.

He asks that I empty myself like one of those stone waterpots at Cana; that I let go of all the old wine that fills my mind; that I join in the dance with him and let the process of transformation unfold over time — his time not mine; that I understand that the miracle of Jesus is not immediate perfection but rather a lifelong process of tripping on the dance floor and getting right back up again.

Like Kisuke was filled with shame and self-doubt, we sometimes hear a voice in our own mind that keeps putting us down; that tries hard to make us stop dancing by telling us that we are not good enough, that we are filled with blemishes, that we are worthless — a voice that keeps trying to change Jesus' wine back into water. But we know that voice is lying. You see, we've been to Cana; we've tasted the wine; we've danced with Jesus — we will never be the same again.

February 1994
Ordinary Time

The Vineyard of Our Life

Luke 13:6-9

And he began telling this parable: "A man had a fig tree which had been planted in his vineyard; and he came looking for fruit on it and did not find any. And he said to the vineyard-keeper, 'Behold, for three years I have come looking for fruit on this fig tree without finding any. Cut it down! Why does it even use up the ground?' And he answered and said to him, 'Let it alone, sir, for this year too, until I dig around it and put in fertilizer; and if it bears fruit next year, fine; but if not, cut it down.'"

*

In biblical times, the fruitful fig tree was symbolic of Israel achieving its highest spiritual potential. For a fig tree to be barren represents a sad loss of what might have been. Each of us is like a fig tree in God's vineyard.

Our loving Creator sends each of us into the world with a very special gift — the potential for forming and maintaining loving relationships with others. And like the fig tree, God plants each of us in a vineyard. We bear fruit when we realize our potential for loving others; we are barren when we are isolated and untouchable.

The vineyard within which we live consists of the multiple roles and responsibilities that we have during the story of our life. Some of us are husbands, fathers, brothers, doctors, teachers or taxi drivers; some are mothers, wives, sisters, attorneys, executives or waitresses. In each of these cases, the role that we play and the responsibilities that go with it offer us the potential for bearing fruit or being barren. What makes the difference is how well we love.

God cares very little about how much money we make or what side of the tracks we live on. When the time comes — and it will in each of our lives — for us to sit side by side with our God and watch the video of our life play out before our eyes, it will only be our relationships with others that really count: how willing were we to forgive; how open to trust; how much risk were we ready to take for those people next to whom God has planted us in the vineyard of life.

Jesus reminds us of this in today's Gospel. When the owner of the vineyard gets fed up with the fig tree's inability to bear fruit, he wants to cut it down. But the vineyard worker asks him to give the tree one more opportunity to bear fruit. "Let it alone, sir, for this year too, until I dig around it and put in fertilizer; and if it bears fruit next year, fine; but if not, then cut it down."

Jesus is the vineyard worker in our life. Perhaps this Lenten season is that one more year that Jesus, our vineyard worker, has asked for on our behalf. Perhaps it is our last chance to bear fruit in our relationships with others before being cut down and carted off by that big DPW truck in the sky. If there are relationships in our lives that have been damaged, let us use this Lenten season to reach out with forgiveness — or contrition — but above all with love to heal those relationships. Let us offer our loving Father in heaven not just 40 days of giving up candy, but a basket full of fruit from the vineyard of our life.

March 2001
Lent

Faith When Life Gets Us Wet

Matthew 14: 24 – 32

(Jesus) made the disciples get into the boat and go ahead of him to the other side . . . He went up on the mountain by himself to pray . . . But the boat was already a long distance from the land, battered by the waves; for the wind was contrary. And in the fourth watch of the night he came to them, walking on the sea. When the disciples saw him walking on the sea, they were terrified, and said, "It is a ghost!" And they cried out in fear. But immediately Jesus spoke to them, saying, "Take courage, it is I; do not be afraid." Peter said to him, "Lord, if it is you, command me to come to you on the water." And he said, "Come!" And Peter got out of the boat, and walked on the water and came toward Jesus. But seeing the wind, he became frightened, and beginning to sink, he cried out, "Lord, save me!" Immediately Jesus stretched out his hand and took hold of him, and said to him, "You of little faith, why did you doubt?"

*

I love Saint Peter. He was a man after my own heart. He was emotional, impulsive, and quick to panic. I can relate to that. Yet Peter was one of Jesus' very best friends. Jesus trusted him so much that he left him in charge; and here we are, twenty centuries later, in Peter's church.

But in his impulsive exuberance in today's Gospel, Peter was expecting Jesus to make magic; to make it possible for him to defy the laws of physics — God's laws of physics — and walk on water.

And when that didn't happen he panicked and started to sink. Our Lord reached out his hand and pulled his friend to safety, "O, you of little faith, why did you doubt?"

Life is a gift, but it's not easy. There are times when things happen around us and to us that can make us panic and even call us to despair: a diagnosis or recurrence of cancer, betrayal by a friend or a spouse, loss of livelihood, death of a loved one, news of a suicide — the list goes on and on. And when these things happen we get wet and, like Peter, we can start to sink. That's when faith comes into play. Jesus never promised magic. He never promised Peter that he wouldn't get wet; he never promised that life wouldn't get us wet. He only promised that he would always be there to pull us safely home to God.

The Jesuit theologian Father John McMurray wrote that those who have an immature, religious faith believe something like this, "Fear not, trust in God, and the things you are afraid of won't happen to you." But those who possess a mature, enduring faith believe much more deeply, "Fear not, trust in God, and the things you are afraid of may happen to you, but you'll get through them with God."

Mature, enduring faith does not expect or wait for magic. It never gives up no matter how wet, how wounded life gets us. It trusts that no matter what happens, somehow, someway, somewhere, whether in this life or in the next, God will make us whole.

The bad things that happen in life are locked in a moment in time. While we are alive we cannot see beyond that locked moment; but our immortal souls are timeless. And somewhere deep in our souls, beyond our fears, beyond our thoughts, our anxieties and grief, there is an intuitive knowledge that in the end God will make everything okay. If that weren't true we wouldn't be here at Mass today.

Let us pray that our faith will continue to mature and endure. And let us always know that Jesus is walking alongside us here in time, walking on the water, holding our hand, bringing us safely home.

August 2008
Ordinary Time

The Road to Emmaus

Luke 24: 13 – 16, 28 – 31, 35

And behold, two of them were going that very day to a village named Emmaus, which was about seven miles from Jerusalem . . . While they were talking and discussing, Jesus himself approached and began traveling with them. But their eyes were prevented from recognizing him . . . And they approached the village where they were going, and he acted as though he were going farther. But they urged him, saying, "Stay with us, for it is getting toward evening, and the day is now nearly over." So he went in to stay with them. When he had reclined at the table with them, he took the bread and blessed it, and breaking it, he began giving it to them. Then their eyes were opened and they recognized him; and he vanished from their sight . . . He was recognized by them in the breaking of the bread.

*

The road to Emmaus is a seven mile journey from Jerusalem; seven miles along a stony broken highway; seven miles from joy to despair.

The two companions traveling that road in today's Gospel were close friends of Jesus. The crucifixion has left them devastated and broken. How could God have allowed this terrible thing to happen to Jesus?

In the depths of their despair they encounter a mysterious stranger who opens their eyes to reveal the presence of Christ. Their depression vanishes along with the mysterious stranger. They turn themselves around and head back to Jerusalem to proclaim the Gospel. It is they who are resurrected.

Some of us have traveled that road to Emmaus. Like many of you, I have struggled with the problem of evil in the world: Why does God whom I love and believe loves each of us permit terrible things to go on: wars, violence of every kind, homelessness, mental illness, incurable disease, natural disaster?

But like those two companions in today's Gospel, I have been blessed. Over and over again my eyes have been opened and I have recognized God in the breaking of the bread of everyday life. I have felt his presence in the chaos and the darkness. And through grace, I have been able to turn myself around and head back to Jerusalem with my faith sustained.

Many years ago I had a powerful Emmaus experience. I had always been a person of faith and hope but some bad things happened. My friend Vic lost his wife and two of their three children when an electrical fire started while they were asleep. Around the same time the young child Etan Patz disappeared on his way to school in New York City and was never seen again. These two events affected me very deeply. I began to ask, where was God?

Shortly after this I began commuting to work in New York City. As I saw the many homeless people suffering and sleeping in the streets and subways, my questioning and doubts increased. Then one day something special happened.

It was a beautiful October morning as I drove down Central Park West. I had been driving in early on Saturday mornings with coffee and sandwiches looking for people who were homeless. I spotted a disheveled young man huddled in a red sweatshirt, sitting on a park bench, rocking back and forth and staring into space. After saying good morning, I offered him some hot coffee, but he didn't respond.

Sitting down on the bench, I poured us both some coffee and placed his cup and a few cookies down next to him. He continued to stare into space. Sipping my coffee I carried on a one-way conversation for a while. He began to chatter in nonsense sounds to each squirrel that ran by.

After a while his fingers inched over to the coffee and he gulped it down as he continued chattering with the squirrels. I finished my second cup of coffee and said good bye, but he still did not acknowledge my presence. Walking to the curb where my car was parked, I kept thinking how this young man was so badly damaged in mind and body that he probably would not survive the winter.

Lost in my own sadness, I pulled away from the curb. As I drove down the street I glanced in my rear view mirror. My friend had left his bench and was standing in the street waving good bye to me.

My eyes welled up with tears; I realized that what I was seeing in my rear view mirror was Christ. Not that this man was Jesus in disguise, but rather that the Christ within him, in the midst of all his brokenness, was reaching out and connecting to the Christ within me. At that instant my eyes were opened and everything made sense.

God places a little piece of himself inside of each of us when we are born. That little piece of God is our immortal soul; it is the Christ within us. Life is the journey of our soul back home to its loving Creator. While our time on earth is limited and the journey can be pretty rough, getting home is all that really matters.

No matter how good we are, how loving, no matter how hard we try, we cannot escape the pain and contradictions of human existence. The symbol of our faith is itself a contradiction: the cross, two opposing beams of wood made from the tree of life — used to torture and destroy life. Yet in the center of the contradiction, we find God in human form.

But the message of the cross is hope. It tells us that we are not alone, that God is with us in the chaos and the darkness; he is present in the pain, loss and disillusionment; he is there at the center of the contradiction, the center of the cross. And someday, once we are free of the constraints of human existence and the limitations of human understanding, it will all make sense; there will be a happy ending, or more truly, a happy beginning — for all eternity.

It is that mysterious stranger, who dwells in the depths of our being — the Christ within each and every one of us — who resurrects US, like he did for those companions on the road to Emmaus, and makes it possible for us to keep turning ourselves around and heading back to Jerusalem.

April 2008
Easter Season

Dropping the Net

Matthew 4: 18 - 20

Now as Jesus was walking by the Sea of Galilee, he saw two brothers, Simon who was called Peter, and Andrew his brother, casting a net into the sea; for they were fishermen. And he said to them, "Follow me, and I will make you fishers of men." Immediately they left their nets and followed him.

*

I have always loved listening to this Gospel story. The imagery is so alive that I can feel myself right there in the boat. I can feel the heat of the sun, hear the seagulls, and smell the ocean. And there is Jesus walking on the shore, smiling, pulling up the hem of his garment as he wades out a bit into the water. He's waving his arm and beckoning to us, "Come follow me."

Hearing this story as a young boy in Catholic school back in the Bronx, I thought it was the greatest adventure that could ever be, better than Robin Hood, better even than Star Trek: to drop everything, leave everything behind; to follow Jesus to the ends of the earth.

But as I got older, fell in love, and raised a family, something about this story began to bother me — what happened to Peter and Andrew's wives and children when they dropped their nets? What about Zebedee, James and John's father, who depended on them to run his fishing business; how did he survive when they climbed out of the boat and went off to follow Jesus?

With maturity has come an understanding that even though they became disciples and followed Jesus, they continued to raise their kids, support their families, and probably went back to work on their fishing boats. But something was different: they had been transformed, changed forever — they had LET GO OF THEIR NETS.

Jesus calls to each and every one of us in a personal way, just like he called to those fishermen in Capernaum. He calls us by name and asks us to follow him; to follow him in the context of our lives and the responsibilities, rooted in love, that are associated with our place in the world.

Jesus calls us to open our hearts and accept God's love; to let it transform us; to let ourselves become channels of God's unconditional love and forgiveness, and to let that love flow through us to all our brothers and sisters, all God's children. He calls us to love and forgive others as God loves and forgives us — unconditionally.

But whatever the circumstances of our lives, if we are to follow Jesus, WE NEED TO DROP OUR NETS. Only our nets are not filled with fish, they are filled with baggage, emotional baggage, collected over a lifetime — anger, hurt, resentment, self-alienation.

Some of us carry heavy, painful, unresolved feelings towards others in our nets: the pain of abandonment as a child by a parent we may have lost through divorce, death, or a debilitating addiction or illness; the hurt of betrayal as an adult by someone we loved and trusted very deeply; anger towards God for an illness or handicap we are traveling through life with, or for taking someone from us in death. The list goes on and on.

Jesus calls us to let go, TO DROP THE NET.

Some of us carry the heavy burden of self-alienation, self-hatred — for not being perfect, for not being someone, anyone, else.

Jesus calls us to let go, TO DROP THE NET.

These feelings are hard to let go of. They are usually the result of very real hurts we have experienced. But if we hold on to them, they are like blockages in the artery of God's love. They stand in the way of our being able to truly love God and love each other; they keep us locked in a prison of bitterness and depression, and make it difficult for God's love to flow through us into the world.

So here we are in Tenafly, 2,000 years later, and we really are in that boat with those fishermen in Capernaum. For whatever the circumstances of our lives, whatever our individual responsibilities, Jesus calls us to be touched by the magic of God's unconditional love. He calls anew as we open our eyes on each brand new day, each new beginning; to drop our net; to let go of the past, of the hurt; to be loved and to love and forgive unconditionally — without strings. He calls us to be healed, he calls us to be whole.

January 1993
Ordinary Time

Out on a Limb

Luke 19: 2 - 10

And there was a man called by the name of Zaccheus; he was a chief tax collector and he was rich. Zaccheus was trying to see who Jesus was, and was unable because of the crowd, for he was small in stature. So he ran on ahead and climbed up into a sycamore tree in order to see him, for he was about to pass through that way. When Jesus came to the place, he looked up and said to him, "Zaccheus, hurry and come down, for today I must stay at your house." And he hurried and came down and received him gladly. When they saw it, they all began to grumble, saying, "He has gone to be the guest of a man who is a sinner." Zaccheus stopped and said to the Lord, "Behold, Lord, half of my possessions I will give to the poor, and if I have defrauded anyone of anything, I will give back four times as much." And Jesus said to him, "Today salvation has come to this house, because he, too, is a son of Abraham. For the Son of Man has come to seek and to save that which was lost."

*

I love hearing this Gospel story. It always makes me smile. I can see the actor Danny DeVito playing the part of Zaccheus, jumping up and down in the crowd, like a pogo stick, trying to catch a glimpse of Jesus. Suddenly a light bulb goes off in his head and he scurries up a tree and out on a limb to see the teacher whom the whole town is talking about: Jesus the miracle worker.

The Gospel tells us that Zaccheus was short in stature, vertically challenged as we would say today with more political correctness. The Gospel tells us that the people disliked him for being a tax collector; that they referred to him as a sinner. But rather than feeling sorry for himself and inadequate, Zaccheus finds a way. He goes out on a limb for Jesus.

And then what happens? This man, who could have gone home feeling unloved and inadequate, pulls himself out on the limb only to find that Jesus has seen him first and is smiling at him and giving him the honor of being his host. "Zaccheus, hurry and come down, for today I must stay at your house." This man who took a risk to catch just a glimpse of Jesus was filled with joy.

There may be some of us who long to welcome Jesus into our heart, into our home, but feel unworthy, inadequate; some who rather than turning outward toward Jesus, rather than going out on a limb, turn inward and fall into the pit of self-loathing and depression.

Whenever we are tempted to do this, we must remember that not only Zaccheus but most, if not all, of the great saints felt unworthy and inadequate. What made them saints was that they did not cave in; they turned their thoughts away from themselves and outward to Jesus. And like Zaccheus, they found to their surprise that Jesus was just waiting for them to welcome him into their homes.

None of us is inadequate. Each of us is adequate; each of us is enough; because each of us is a beloved child of God. We will miss out on the joy of locking eyes with Jesus if we hold ourselves back from taking a risk; if we decide to go home rather than out on a limb.

November 2007
Ordinary Time

Why Not

Matthew 5:38 - 39, 43 – 44

"You have heard that it was said, 'An eye for an eye, and a tooth for a tooth.' But I say to you, do not resist an evil person; but whoever slaps you on your right cheek, turn the other to him also . . . You have heard that it was said, 'You shall love your neighbor and hate your enemy.' But I say to you, love your enemies and pray for those who persecute you . . ."

*

No resistance. Turn the other cheek. Love your enemies. I can almost hear Saint Peter's shocked reaction, "Jesus, give me a break!"

Was Jesus kidding? Was he just being idealistic or poetic? Did he not expect anyone to take him at his word? If the answer to these questions is 'yes', then Jesus might be remembered as a terrific 1st century stand-up comic, or as a wise social philosopher — a sort of Jewish Confucius. But Jesus is neither of these; he is the human voice of God and I think he meant what he said.

However, there's more than one way to turn the other cheek.

Turning the other cheek doesn't have to mean accepting abuse, letting ourselves or others be slapped around or victimized. Turning the other cheek can mean NOT turning away: forever bouncing back; living in a world filled with pain and suffering, greed and violence, yet never giving up on making it different, on building a world filled with love and goodness — a place that Jesus called the Kingdom.

Robert Kennedy frequently quoted from George Bernard Shaw, "Some see things as they are and ask, 'why'. I see things as they could be and ask, 'why not?'" Jesus asks us to turn the other cheek; to forever bounce back; to be people of the 'why not' not the 'why'; to look in the face of a troubled and hurt-filled world, and then to look into our own lives. He asks us to take inventory of the talents and skills that we possess, and to ask, 'why not'; and then to turn the other cheek, bounce back, and make a decision to use those talents and skills to reduce the pain and suffering. He asks us to be channels for God's love to enter into and to change the world.

Mother Teresa was a 40 year old teacher in an exclusive boarding school for the daughters of wealthy expatriates living in India. She saw and was touched by the suffering of the poor dying in the streets of Calcutta. She left the comfort of her life and began a ministry of loving and caring for the poorest of the poor, enabling them to die with dignity. She saw suffering, asked, 'why not', turned the other cheek and bounced back.

A homemaker and mother living in Bergen County was moved by the tragic statistics of abortion in the United States. She began taking unwed mothers into her home, and set up a network of resources to help young, pregnant women who felt that they had no alternative to abortion. She asked, 'why not', turned the other cheek and bounced back.

A very successful plastic surgeon, a friend whom I admire very much, was moved by the plight of children in third world countries who suffer deformities as well as poverty. He began organizing teams of doctors and nurses, and has made several trips to these countries performing corrective surgery in makeshift operating rooms on thousands of children. He asked, 'why not', turned the other cheek and bounced back.

A young man in Oregon, who had lost both legs in an accident, learned how to play basketball from a wheelchair. He reached out to handicapped, inner-city kids, and formed a basketball league giving them the gifts of athletics and self-esteem.

All these people saw pain and suffering in the world and asked, 'why not'. Instead of turning away in despair, they turned the other cheek and bounced back. They decided to use their talents and skills to put God's love and their own faith into action to change the world.

Some days I read the papers or watch the news with horror — the senseless violence and cruelty that randomly destroys innocent lives; the tragedies of racism, sexism, anti-Semitism, homophobia, war, abortion, AIDS, substance abuse. I am tempted to turn away in despair; to throw my fists up to heaven and scream, 'WHY?' — to blame God for allowing another tragedy.

But then I remember Jesus, and the reality that God calls each of us by name, and asks us to be his human hands and feet in this world. And I ask myself, 'WHY NOT?'

February 1993
Ordinary Time

Casting the First Stone

John 8: 3 – 11

The scribes and the Pharisees brought a woman caught in adultery, and having set her in the center of the court, they said to (Jesus), "Teacher, this woman has been caught in adultery, in the very act. Now in the Law Moses commanded us to stone such women; what then do you say?" They were saying this, testing him, so that they might have grounds for accusing him. But Jesus stooped down and with his finger wrote on the ground. But when they persisted in asking him, he straightened up, and said to them, "He who is without sin among you, let him be the first to throw a stone at her." Again he stooped down and wrote on the ground. When they heard it, they began to go out one by one, beginning with the older ones, and he was left alone, and the woman, where she was, in the center of the court. Straightening up, Jesus said to her, "Woman, where are they? Did no one condemn you?" She said, "No one, Lord." And Jesus said, "I do not condemn you, either. Go. From now on sin no more."

*

God is not a man or a woman. God is not a Christian or a Jew or a Muslim or a Hindu or a Buddhist. God is love; pure unconditional love. When we experience unconditional love, we are in the presence of God. When we love someone unconditionally God is acting through us.

We try to represent God in words and pictures; in symbols and stained glass windows. But God cannot be framed in mental images. God cannot be described in human words. The only thing we can know with certainty about God is what Saint John tells us in the Gospel: God is love; and he or she who abides in love, abides in God.

The presence of God in our lives is not measured by how many Masses we attend, or rosaries we pray. It's not dependent on the acts of religious piety we practice, or the politics we subscribe to. It's not observable by the color of our skin, our religious affiliation, our place in society, our marital status or our sexual orientation. The presence of God in our lives is dependent on one thing only — the presence of unconditional love in our hearts. Someone once asked Jesus what the greatest commandment is — what the most important thing is that we were called to do with our lives. His answer was very clear: "Love God with your whole heart and soul and love your neighbor as yourself."

The people in today's Gospel were very self-righteous and unloving. They saw themselves as God's avenging agents, but Jesus very gently set them straight. He bent down and wrote with his finger in the dirt. One by one he looked into their eyes and wrote down each person's private sins, their acts of meanness and selfishness. He showed them how far from God they were. And one by one they dropped their stones and slipped away with shame. Then Jesus lifted the frightened woman from the ground. He showed her unconditional love and she experienced the presence of God. She went away both forgiven and healed.

Are there times when we are tempted to look down on others; to feel that we are morally superior or closer to God; to think that another person is unworthy to receive Communion; times when our hands are raised to cast the stones of self-righteousness? As we approach the end of Lent, let us pause and feel Jesus' finger writing gently on our hearts; reminding us of our own humanness; calling us to stop judging others; calling us to drop our stones; calling us to love and forgive others the way God loves and forgives us.

March 2007
Lent

Blessed Are We

John 20:19 – 21, 24 – 29

So when it was evening on that day, the first day of the week, and when the doors were shut where the disciples were, for fear . . . Jesus came and stood in their midst . . . He showed them both his hands and his side. The disciples then rejoiced when they saw the Lord. But Thomas, one of the twelve, called Didymus, was not with them when Jesus came. So the other disciples were saying to him, "We have seen the Lord!" But he said to them, "Unless I see in his hands the imprint of the nails, and put my finger into the place of the nails, and put my hand into his side, I will not believe." . . . After eight days his disciples were again inside, and Thomas with them. Jesus came, the doors having been shut, and stood in their midst and said, "Peace be with you." Then he said to Thomas, "Reach here with your finger, and see my hands; and reach here your hand and put it into my side; and do not be unbelieving, but believing." Thomas answered and said to him "My Lord and my God!" Jesus said to him, "Because you have seen me, have you believed? Blessed are they who did not see, and yet believed."

*

I heard someone once say that it was Jesus' friends who came back to life at Easter; that it was Peter and John and Mary Magdalene and Thomas and the rest of his disciples who rose from the tomb of despair and doubt; that what God sent walking out of that empty tomb was the gift of faith — faith that doesn't require proof to sustain it, faith that lives on 2,000 years later inside of each one of us here at Mass today.

How many of us have ever hit rock bottom? Ever felt that there was no hope, that we couldn't push ourselves any further, that we couldn't face ourselves in the mirror? How many have ever begged God to change a bad situation, or asked for a sign, some proof that he was really there, that everything would be ok?

Well that's what's happening to Thomas and the other disciples in today's Gospel. They are huddled together in fear in the back room of some house in Jerusalem, each one probably making plans to leave town and forget they ever knew each other or Jesus.

Thomas is not only the star of this story, but I think, in a way, he represents us at points in our lives. He's been through a terrible experience. Not only has he lost Jesus but he is probably overcome with shame and guilt for having turned his back and run away when Jesus was arrested. He thinks that the only way things could be alright again would be for God to send him a sign, some proof, the chance to touch the wounds of Jesus. But just when he's about to give up he experiences the presence of Jesus within himself. And then something amazing happens: he no longer needs a miracle — he passes on the chance to touch the nail marks of Jesus. Nothing has changed, yet everything has changed — his faith is resurrected. In the end what brings Thomas' faith back to life is not the proof that he thought he needed, but rather his personal experience of the Risen Christ.

How many times have we been filled with doubt or anxiety and huddled in some back room like the disciples in today's Gospel? How many times have we faced grief or hurt or loss: perhaps the death of a loved one, or betrayal by a friend, or maybe positive results from a biopsy? But what sets us apart as modern day disciples of Jesus is that little piece of Thomas that lives within each of us — that part of our soul that refuses to give in to despair; that part of our mind that no longer demands proof.

We are those blessed ones whom Jesus refers to in the Gospel: We are those who have not seen Jesus and have still believed. We can look on as the Eucharist is elevated at the Consecration of the Mass and say with the same certainty as Thomas, *"My Lord and My God."* And we can do this because over and over again, day after day, year after year, no matter how many times we may hit rock bottom, we experience Christ alive in our hearts. And if that weren't true, we wouldn't be here at Mass. We'd be home in bed, or out to dinner, or someplace else.

But we're not, we're here — we chose to come to Mass.

Blessed are we who have not seen and yet still believe!

April 2006
Easter Season

That Was Me

The Gospel of Saint Matthew contains a parable in which Jesus lays out the bottom line of what it means to be a Christian and how our lifetime behavior will ultimately be evaluated. It is Jesus' parable of the last judgment where Christ the King comes in glory to separate the sheep from the goats:

> *"Then he will also say to those on his left, 'Depart from me, accursed ones . . . for I was hungry, and you gave me nothing to eat; I was thirsty, and you gave me nothing to drink; I was a stranger, and you did not invite me in; naked, and you did not clothe me; sick, and in prison, and you did not visit me.' Then they themselves also will answer, 'Lord, when did we see you hungry, or thirsty, or a stranger, or naked, or sick, or in prison, and did not take care of you?' Then he will answer them, 'Truly I say to you, to the extent that you did not do it to one of the least of these, you did not do it to me.'"*

Matthew 25: 41-44.

*

Jesus wasn't kidding around when he said this. He meant it for the people around him; and he meant it for us. Many religions preach the Golden Rule — do unto others as you would have them do unto you. But Jesus, Our Savior, the one we believe is God made man to redeem us, went way beyond the Golden Rule: love unconditionally, forgive unconditionally, turn your other cheek when someone strikes you, and treat every human being as if he or she were me. These are the instructions that Jesus handed down over 2,000 years of history to each and every one of us.

And this is what makes Christianity different from every religion and every philosophy. This is what being a Christian, a disciple of Jesus, is about. It's not just about worship; it's not just about dogma; it's not just concerned with issues of human sexuality. It's about unconditional love and forgiveness even at the cost of one's comfort, even at the cost of one's personal or national pride, even at the cost of one's life. It's about treating the least, most vulnerable, most unlovable, most disenfranchised member of society just like we would treat Jesus himself. Jesus wasn't kidding around when he said this. His message was hard to hear back then, and it's hard to hear today.

The Catholic Social Teaching of our popes and our bishops has always been very strong and very clear. Christians are called to a life of charity towards the poor. But that's not where it ends — we are called to a life of advocacy as well. We are called not just to give generously of our means but to stand up for, protect and be a voice for the poor, the vulnerable, and the disenfranchised:

> *"Truly I say to you, to the extent that you did not do it to one of the least of these, you did not do it to me."*

The Church calls on us to be pure of heart and deed, but it also calls on us to reject the structures of sin in our society and to promote a seamless culture of life. It's sometimes easier to define and fixate on sin as consisting of sexual acts than to recognize the sin inherent in poverty, neglect, discrimination, racism, anti-Semitism. It's sometimes easier to be a vocal advocate for the unborn than to be a vocal advocate for the residents of death row. But Jesus wasn't kidding around; and he wasn't just making suggestions.

After hearing the parable of the sheep and the goats, can't we see Jesus standing with Cardinal Mahoney of Los Angeles in opposition to a proposed law that would make it a crime to feed and shelter illegal immigrants? Can't we see him standing for a compassionate form of controlled amnesty for illegal immigrants who have worked and paid taxes here for many years so that they can make a better life for their families? If Jesus were sick would we find him being cared for by the best nurses and physicians at Hackensack University Medical Center, New York Presbyterian, Englewood Medical Center, Memorial Sloan Kettering; or would he be waiting in line at some charity clinic with the forty four million Americans who have no access to healthcare?

Wouldn't Jesus have stood with Pope John Paul II when he called for an end to the death penalty? Wouldn't he support Pope Benedict XVI's statement, which I quote, ". . . the concept of preventive war does not appear in *The Catechism of the Catholic Church."*?

If Jesus were interviewed on the Sunday talk shows, what would he say about collateral damage, about prisoner abuse; how would he feel about the genocide in Darfur, about injustices in the refugee camps of the Middle East? What would he think about members of Congress, in both parties, who have the best health benefits for themselves and their families, vote themselves regular pay raises, pass huge tax cuts for the wealthiest members of society, but can't manage to pass a $2.15 increase to the minimum wage?

Jesus wasn't kidding around — he calls us to a life of charity but he calls us to a life of advocacy as well.

And, my sisters and brothers, this isn't personal opinion, this isn't politics — this is the teaching of our popes and bishops; this is the teaching of our Roman Catholic Church. That fact notwithstanding, it ain't easy. If you are like me, you struggle with these complex moral issues.

Mount Carmel is a very generous parish family. We are a tithing parish and annually support a Catholic Worker House, an AIDS hospice, and Christian base communities in Peru. Teams of our parish volunteers are involved in various outreach ministries: operating a food pantry; soliciting manufacturers, distributors and vendors for excess supplies of diapers, baby clothes, toys, etc. and distributing these items to needy families; cooking and delivering meals to a homeless shelter; and visiting the sick and imprisoned. These are wonderful acts of charity, but how will we answer the Church's call to *advocacy*? If you would like to be part of discerning that answer, we invite you to a workshop to discuss the Catholic Social Teaching of our U.S. bishops, and how we as individuals and as a parish might answer the call to advocacy. Please check the bulletin for dates, time and place.

That parable of Jesus in Matthew's Gospel — the one about the sheep and the goats — has been adapted for twenty first century American ears by Jesuit Father James Hug, president of the Center for Concern in Washington, D.C. I found it powerful when I read it. It made me confront hypocrisy in my own life; it made me look at how I need to change my behavior. I'd like to share it with you:

"Then Christ will say to those on his left [the goats]: 'Out of my sight . . .' [They will ask him when was it that they treated him so badly?] . . . and he will answer them: when you turned away as my hunger turned to malnutrition and starvation, while you overate and overfed your pets . . .when you, who came here as poor immigrants, began scapegoating new immigrants . . . when you stuffed your closets

with more clothes than you need . . . when you rested secure with good health insurance for your family, while fighting universal coverage and funding for public health services for we who are mired in poverty . . . when you were willing to pour out money for prisons but not for the neighborhood programs, schools and jobs that could have reduced the need for prisons . . . I truly say to you, that's when you did it to me."

September 2006
Feast of Christ the King

The Video of Our Life

Recently I completed two family projects that I've wanted to do for a long time. For the first project I took the best photographs from 65 albums of family pictures taken over the years and digitized them onto one three hour DVD with background music. For the second project I edited close to 40 family video tapes onto one four hour and 20 minute *Ferrauiola Family Video Special.* The DVD begins with photos of my wife's and my parents and our individual childhoods. It goes on through our teen years, our high school romance, the early years of our marriage, the arrival of each of our four children, and all the special moments of our life together over the last thirty five years. The video captures the personalities of the six of us, our senses of humor and spontaneity. It begins when our youngest daughter is only one and progresses up to the present, twenty years later.

Sitting with my wife Wanda in our family room and watching the DVD and the video is a real joy for me. Seeing our marriage and our children weave and grow together over the years fills me with thanksgiving for my family and for my life. But along with the joyful times there have been difficult days: the challenges of raising four children, of work, of illness. I'm sure that if I could zero in and drill down to many of the days and see scenes that didn't make it to the camera, I would see moments of anxiety and doubt. But sitting in the family room with my arm around Wanda, smiling and laughing as we watch 38 years of life and love roll by the TV screen, it's clear that God's grace has always been with us.

Now think of your life and the life of every person who has ever lived and will live in the future, and of all the DVDs and videos that could be made from all those individual stories. What if they were made and someone edited those billions of DVDs and videos into one big video called *The Story of the Human Family*. And what if someday, after we have died, gone to heaven and been reunited with our loved ones, God gets us all together in his big family room in heaven, to watch this *Story of the Human Family*?

As we watch the history of civilization unfold we would see moments of goodness, love, sacrifice and heroism. Sadly, we would also see moments of pain, war, horror and shame. But sitting with our loved ones in the eternal presence of God, beyond the limits of our time here on earth, we would know that God's grace had carried us through.

But we're not there yet; and that's where faith comes in. You see here we are in 2003 and we are still making the movie, shooting the videos of our life and the life of the human family. We may be in the middle of a happy time or a painful time; we don't know what tomorrow will bring and we certainly don't know how the story will end. But we are here at Mass today because we have faith. We trust that no matter what difficulties and tragedies befall us as individuals or as society as a whole, they are only moments isolated in time. We believe that in the long run — either in this life or the next — God's grace will pull us through and fix whatever has been broken.

Some day we will gather in God's eternal family room together with our loved ones, the ones here now and the ones who have left us, and we will watch a wonderful story, the story of our journey home.

August 2003
Ordinary Time

Lazarus and the Problem of Evil

John 11: 1, 3, 5, 17, 32, 35, 43

Now a certain man was sick, Lazarus of Bethany, the village of Mary and her sister Martha . . . the sisters sent word to (Jesus), saying, "Lord, behold, he whom you love is sick." . . . Now Jesus loved Martha and her sister and Lazarus . . . So when Jesus came, he found that he had already been in the tomb four days . . . when Mary came where Jesus was, she saw him, and fell at his feet, saying to him, "Lord, if you had been here, my brother would not have died." . . . Jesus wept . . . he cried out with a loud voice, "Lazarus, come forth."

*

I had prayed every day for Daniel Pearl, the reporter for the Wall Street Journal who had been kidnapped by terrorists in Pakistan; for his wife and his yet to be born baby. When I heard the news that he had been brutally murdered and butchered, I felt like my own brother had been killed. *Lord, if you had been here, my brother would not have died.*

A little girl named Danielle Van Damme was abducted from her bedroom and her body was found weeks later. Over 3,000 lives were stolen on September 11th and many thousands upon thousands of other lives and hearts were forever broken. *Lord, if you had been here, my brothers and my sisters would not have died.*

Why does our all powerful, all loving God permit such evil to exist? God gives each of us real freedom to choose goodness over darkness. Some of his children choose the darkness and, as a result, bad things — terrible things — happen. The consequences of those bad things are for us a never ending nightmare. But in God's reality they are only a nanosecond in time compared to the eternity that God has waiting for us.

Look at today's Gospel: Lazarus lay dead for four days in a tomb. His sisters could not understand how their best friend Jesus, the miracle worker, could have let it happen. *Lord, if you had been here my brother would not have died.* Every minute of those four days was an eternity of suffering for Martha and Mary. In the end Jesus brings Lazarus back to life; and those four days of horror become a distant, faded memory compared to the joy of being reunited.

And that is how it will be for us. The four days in the tomb are like life here on earth. The pain felt by Martha and Mary is like the pain we experience in dealing with the presence of evil in our world. But in God's eye all of it is temporary — like the four days that Lazarus lay dead in his tomb. There is so very much more that God has waiting for us.

But God isn't just waiting in the wings for us to run the gauntlet of life. He is here, present with us in the darkness, suffering with us in the face of unspeakable evil, weeping for us like he wept for Lazarus. And we know this is true when we look upon the cross. In the center of the cross, in the center of suffering and evil, we find God in human form.

With the cross, God is sending us an answer to the problem of evil. He is telling us that we are not alone, that he is with us through it all; and someday it will all make sense. And all the people we have lost in our lives, perhaps our parents, perhaps our children; all those who have been so dear to us — all the Daniel Pearls, all the Danielle Van Dammes, all the victims of hatred and bigotry and war and terror will share with us in the joy of God's presence for all eternity.

March 2002
Lent

We Are the Church

Acts 2: 1 – 2, 4

When the day of Pentecost had come, they were all together in one place. And suddenly there came from heaven a noise like a violent rushing wind, and it filled the whole house where they were sitting. . . And they were all filled with the Holy Spirit.

*

Michael Jackson gave us a hit song a few years back,

We are the World,
We are the Children,
We are the ones to make a brighter day.

That song is very fitting today, the feast of Pentecost; because, by virtue of our Baptism, each one of us can paraphrase Michael Jackson and say,

We are the Church,
We are the Body of Christ,
We are the ones to build the Kingdom of God.

Pentecost is the day we celebrate the birthday of the Church, but not everyone comes to the party happy. Many don't even show up anymore. For some the Church has changed too much and too quickly; for others, the change hasn't been fast enough.

In times of frustration, it's tempting to think of the Church as something out there — some monolithic superstructure over which we have little control. But the Church is not some abstract reality that lives behind Vatican walls. The Church is you, and the Church is me struggling to follow as the Holy Spirit guides us through history. And the Church of the 21st and the 25th centuries will be the beneficiary of what we do in our lifetimes to help it grow.

As a child I listened with awe to the story of Pentecost: the Apostles huddled in fear in the upper room; the doors fly open; the Holy Spirit appears; tongues of fire descend upon the Apostles turning their fear to courage. They take to the streets, shouting for joy for all the world to hear, "Jesus Christ is Lord. He has risen!" And so the Church was born.

The child in me that listened with awe to this wonderful story grew up believing that the Apostles and the Church they created were perfect — incapable of human weakness, of discord, controversy, or sin. But with maturity has come an understanding that the Church didn't land in the streets of Jerusalem on Pentecost Day as a perfect, finished product. The Church is being guided through history by the Holy Spirit; but the operative word is 'guided' — not dragged, not coerced.

As such, the Church is like a flower or a human being — it is a living, growing organism. And, like each of us, it is called to perfection but is capable of weakness and failure along the way. But like us, it is called to get back up each time that it falls; and to never give up on becoming all that it is called to be.

We are the Church,
We are the Body of Christ,
We are the ones to build the Kingdom of God.

The Apostles didn't ride off into the sunset on Pentecost to live perfectly harmonious and stress-free lives. The Church in those early days was very much like the Church of today. There was tremendous faith and love, but there was also controversy, differences of opinion and struggle for growth.

The first Christian community in Jerusalem was headed by Saint James. It consisted of Jewish followers of the Gospel who continued to observe strict kosher dietary laws. Eventually Gentiles joined the community. They came from all parts of the Mediterranean and all cultures. Being Gentiles, they did not follow kosher restrictions on what they could eat.

In this first Christian parish, the Eucharist was celebrated at the end of a common meal. Preparing the menu for this meal presented political problems for the community. The Jewish members, who were in the majority, wanted to stick with tradition and serve only kosher food. The Gentiles didn't want to abandon their ethnic eating customs for fear of losing their cultural identity. Both groups lobbied Saint Peter, our first Pope, but he was evasive and indecisive. He wanted to welcome the Gentiles to share the Eucharist with no dietary restrictions, but he feared the backlash from the Jewish members. So he just stopped eating with the Gentiles. This caused tremendous hurt, and created tension between the two groups.

To avert the breakdown of the community, the Council of Jerusalem — our very first Church council — was called. Saint Paul argued powerfully against Saint James while Saint Peter sat in arbitration. Paul's position was accepted by the elders of the community, and the kosher dietary laws were abandoned. The community could henceforth celebrate the Eucharist together. By this decision the Church became truly universal — no longer tied exclusively to the Jewish religion.

Of course, this could have had a different ending. James or Paul or the Gentiles could have turned their backs on the community, and gone off to do their own thing. But they didn't; they let the Holy Spirit guide them through the storm. And, as a result, here we sit, 2,000 years later — one culturally diverse community, preparing to celebrate that same Eucharist.

We are the Church,
We are the Body of Christ,
We are the ones to build the Kingdom of God.

The Church of the 14th century got into a real mess. The Pope moved from Rome to Avignon, France and then back to Rome again. But the French Cardinals didn't want to go back to Rome — so they elected their own Pope. The two Popes excommunicated each other. The Christian world was polarized, and torn by politics and confusion.

Saint Catherine of Sienna, a great doctor of the Church, argued forcefully in defense of the Italian Pope against Saint Vincent Ferrer, a gifted Dominican preacher, who strongly supported the Pope in Avignon. Catherine prevailed and won Vincent over to her position. The French Pope fled into the night, thereby averting a permanent split in the Church. Of course, this could have had a different ending: Catherine or Vincent could have turned their backs and walked away disillusioned with the Church. But they didn't. They let the Holy Spirit guide them through the storm and, as a result, here we sit 700 years later — one community under one Holy Father.

We are the Church,
We are the Body of Christ,
We are the ones to build the Kingdom of God.

Vatican II in the 1960s was a wonderful movement of the Holy Spirit. But some have walked away. Some, because the movement was too fast: too much change too quickly; they long for the security of tradition — the Latin Mass, meatless Fridays. Others have walked away because the movement was too slow: too little change, too long to wait.

This latter group almost included me. In 1987, I dropped out of the formation program for deacons. I long for the day when all my sisters around the world, my daughters, and my wife are invited to participate in ordained ministry. Church history was moving too slowly for me on this issue. Not only did I withdraw from the diaconate program, but for many months I struggled with the question of whether I could remain a member of the Church. But then I remembered Paul, James and the Gentiles, Catherine of Sienna and Vincent Ferrer; and I realized that for change and growth to happen, I couldn't walk away — I had to be here to be part of the process. I let the Holy Spirit guide me through my storm; and here I am, six years later, sharing my hopes and dreams for the future of our Church with you, my parish family.

We are the Church,
We are the Body of Christ,
We are the ones to build the Kingdom of God.

The Church isn't out there, it's in here. It's this lady in the second row; it's Sister Suzanne and Father Ashley; it's the baby we baptized last week; it's Pope John Paul II, and Archbishop McCarrick; it's my friend Bob, with whom I shared the Eucharist many times in his hospital room before he died of AIDS; it's the young mother from Closter who lost her baby, her family and her home to a heroin addiction, and sits begging for food in the Port Authority Bus Terminal.

The Church is you, and the Church is me. For change and growth to happen, we need to be here — to use our gifts and our talents to help move the institutional church wherever it is that the Holy Spirit is leading us.

We are members of the Body of Christ; but each and every one of us IS the Body of Christ. We are Eucharist to each other and to the world; we are the world; we are the Church; we are the future.

May 1993
Pentecost

All Saints

Halloween: It isn't just a day for good little witches and goblins to ring doorbells and collect candy. It's All Hallows Eve, the Eve of All Saints Day — a feast that hopefully will include you and me someday, since God has graciously invited each one of us to the party.

*

Human beings need heroes, role models that we can look up to and say, "I want to be like him or her. They did it, so I guess it's possible for me to do it too!"

Unfortunately, many of our heroes don't last too long. It seems like every day we get bombarded with new opportunities for disillusionment: a Congresswoman we admired is indicted for bribery and extortion; a sports figure who has given hope and pride to millions of young people is convicted of rape; a priest who has given peace and guidance to his parish for many years is arrested for indecent exposure.

As mature and compassionate people, we try to understand and forgive the weaknesses of our public figures; but it hurts and can tempt us to lose faith in others and, more tragically, in our own potential.

It's a lot easier for us to be discouraged by these living, wayward role models than to be encouraged and inspired by those role models we call saints. We tend to see ourselves more prone to human frailty like these flesh and blood figures we read about in the *New York Times*, than to holiness like some distant saint from a faraway time and place.

Maybe that's because we've made the saints untouchable. Some of that is due to remoteness — let's face it, they're dead. But some of it may be because we've mythologized the saints: made them into something that we ourselves can never be — perfect. But if we look closely, we just might notice how much like us they were. And once we notice that, we just might realize how much like them we are called to be.

But what is a saint? For openers, they were real live flesh and blood human beings like you and me. They all had hopes and dreams, fears and self doubts, good days and bad days like we do. They made mistakes; they may have been selfish and petty at times. They were people with all the imperfections, troubles, and joys that we ourselves experience. They would understand our struggles because they themselves have been through them.

We need to take the saints down from the pedestals and the dashboards that we've put them on, and bring them into our everyday lives. That way, they can become touchable to us. We can look at them and say, "I want to be like him or her. They did it so I know that I can do it too!"

I have always found Saint Peter to be most encouraging. He was a man after my own heart. He was emotional, impulsive and often indecisive. He shouted his undying loyalty to Jesus barely twelve hours before he pretended that he never knew him. But Peter, unlike Judas, kept scraping himself up off the floor each time that he failed. Each time he felt remorse, but recommitted himself anew to Jesus from his heart. But his human nature kept getting in his way. After being forgiven over and over again, and given the responsibility of being the rock of Jesus' church, he still made mistakes.

As legend has it, Peter was making a quick getaway from Rome while Nero was executing his parishioners. He happened to run into his conscience — in the form of Jesus — on the Appian Way. Jesus asked him a question, "Quo Vadis? Where are you going, Peter?" And Peter, remorseful, once more recommitted himself. He turned around, returned to Rome and to martyrdom.

Saint Peter was one of Jesus' very best friends; and today, twenty centuries later, he is one of our greatest saints. But, you know something? He was far from perfect — right up to the end.

God is calling you and me to be saints. The word 'saint' comes from the Latin word 'sanctus' which means 'holy'. And 'holy' with an 'h' really means 'wholly' with a 'wh'.

God wants us to be *whole*, to eventually get it all together. But he wants us to realize that this will probably never happen during our lifetime on earth; that we, like the greatest of saints, are human and will continue to have good days and bad days.

Instead, God asks us to commit ourselves to the process of BECOMING whole: to live our lives with a fundamental option for goodness, compassion, forgiveness, and unconditional love; to keep renewing and recommitting ourselves to that option each time we fall. God asks us to look at the saints and to say, "I can do it too!"

God is calling us to be All Saints. He graciously invites us to participate in the feast. And he's really counting on us to make it to the party.

November 1993
All Saints Day

Blindness

John 9: 1, 6 – 8, 10 – 11, 13 – 16, 18 – 19, 24 – 25, 34

As (Jesus) passed by, he saw a man blind from birth . . . He spat on the ground, and made clay of the spittle, and applied the clay to his eyes, and said to him, "Go, wash in the pool of Siloam" (which is translated, 'Sent'). So he went away and washed, and came back seeing. Therefore the neighbors, and those who previously saw him as a beggar, were saying, "Is not this the one who used to sit and beg?" . . . So they were saying to him, "How then were your eyes opened?" He answered, "The man who is called Jesus made clay, and anointed my eyes, and said to me, 'Go to Siloam and wash'; so I went away and washed, and I received sight." . . . They brought to the Pharisees the man who was formerly blind. Now it was a Sabbath on the day when Jesus made the clay and opened his eyes. Then the Pharisees also were asking him again how he received his sight. And he said to them, "He applied clay to my eyes, and I washed, and I see." Therefore some of the Pharisees were saying, "This man is not from God, because he does not keep the

Sabbath" . . . they called the parents of the very one who had received his sight, and questioned them, saying, "Is this your son, who you say was born blind? Then how does he now see?" . . . So a second time they called the man who had been blind, and said to him, "Give glory to God; we know that this man is a sinner." He then answered, "Whether he is a sinner, I do not know; one thing I do know, that though I was blind, now I see." . . . They answered him, "You were born entirely in sin, and are you teaching us?" So they put him out.

*

Knowing and seeing the truth can be hazardous to your lifestyle. It can lead to behavioral changes that maybe we'd rather not make. So sometimes we resist the opportunity to know; we pretend not to see; we try real hard not to understand, not to feel.

Jesus' curing of the blind man is a wonderful story. While it appeals to us on one level, it's really calling us to action on another. In the story Jesus gives a precious gift. This man, who has never seen, opens his eyes for the very first time. The appeal is in the magic, the joy, the miracle that happens; but that's not the end of it. Jesus brings this man out of the darkness and into the light for a purpose. He calls him forth and sends him into action: "Go wash in the pool of Siloam" (which means the one who has been sent).

The man's life gets very complicated from that point forward. No one is happy for him. For some reason, society is threatened by him now. Everyone is hostile and using him as a reference point to attack Jesus. Even his parents distance themselves from him. As a blind beggar, at least he belonged; but now society chews him up and tries to spit him out. The more he stands up for Jesus, the more he is degraded and abused until finally he suffers bodily harm. The Gospel writer doesn't tell us the man's name. Perhaps he is meant to represent everyman, everywoman. Perhaps he is meant to be you and me.

Where Jesus used spit and mud to give sight to the blind man, he uses the Gospel — handed down through the centuries — to give sight to us. But once we are brought into the light, our life too can get complicated, for the Gospel calls us to action.

What exactly is it that we Christians are called to do? Jesus tells us in one special parable, the story of the Last Judgment. He tells us about the confusion among those people who are not being admitted into heaven: "Lord, when did we see you hungry and not offer you food; naked and not offer to clothe you? When were you lonely and we didn't spend time with you. When did we see you cry and not try to wipe away your tears?" The Lord answers: "I tell you, each time you neglected to do these things for the very least of your sisters and brothers, you neglected to do them for me."

What complications has Jesus' gift of sight caused in our lives?

Seeing as Christians in the light of the Gospel: how can we climb over the bodies of homeless people as we commute each day to work, and avoid seeing the face of Christ in each one of them? And once we do see, what do we do then?

Seeing as Christians in the light of the Gospel: how can we fail to recognize Christ in the lonely and hurting eyes of the spouse we have neglected in our quest for self-fulfillment; the children who've grown up while we were out building our career or doing our thing; the relative or friend we haven't spoken to for years over some incident we can't even remember? And once we do see, what do we do then?

Seeing as Christians in the light of the Gospel: how do we miss the Christ standing in the shadows who listens and watches with sadness as we buy into gossip; as we accept, by our silence, the racially or ethnically degrading joke, the anti-Semitic or homophobic remark? And once we do see, what do we do then?

The answer to these questions is very personal and different for each one of us. But once we recognize conflict between our lifestyle and the Gospel, once we see Christ present in each of our sisters and brothers, we are called to make decisions, to act — to fail to do so is to pretend not to see. And everyone knows that, thanks to Jesus, we Christians can now see.

If someday in our world being a Christian were to become a crime, let us hope that there would be enough evidence to convict each and every one of us, and to put us away for eternity.

March 1993
Lent

Our Fathers

Jesus gave us a wonderful gift. He brought God into the center of our lives, and gave us the image of him as a loving father — *Our Father who art in heaven.* But what happens to our image of God when the word 'father' brings up painful memories, unresolved feelings? Father's Day is a good day to reflect on what that image means in our lives. Father's Day is a very good day for forgiveness and for healing.

*

In Aramaic, the language Jesus spoke, the word 'Abba' means 'daddy' or 'papa'. It is a loving term that conjures up all that is wonderful about a father. Jesus taught us to call God 'Abba'.

The English language translation of the New Testament loses some of the meaning intended by Jesus in the original Aramaic. *Our Father who art in heaven* is very nice, and much more personal than 'Yahweh'; but our 'Daddy' conveys a sense of trust and vulnerability, a feeling of unconditional love and acceptance that gets a little lost when 'Abba' is translated as 'father'.

It wasn't an accident that Jesus chose this imagery to describe God. For better or worse, whether present or absent, functional or dysfunctional, our fathers may very well be the most influential people in our lives. And, to a large extent, our emotional and spiritual growth, as well as the way we feel towards God, depends on how we ultimately come to terms with the feelings we have for our fathers.

Jesus wanted us to think of God as a loving father. He gave us this image to help us open ourselves more fully to God's unconditional love and acceptance. But how do we begin to believe that God, our heavenly father, loves and accepts us unconditionally if our earthly father didn't or couldn't?

Many of us carry around some painful childhood memories about our fathers. Perhaps a sense of loss or abandonment by a father who wasn't physically or emotionally present for us due to a divorce, an untimely death, a debilitating illness or addiction, a suicide. Maybe we carry a feeling that no matter what we did, or how hard we tried, we weren't acceptable or lovable enough to get our father's approval, to make him happy, to make him stay. Perhaps we bear the scars of physical, emotional, or sexual abuse. Maybe he even gave us away.

These painful experiences often stay hidden away in our subconscious mind — too painful to confront. While there, they are like blockages in the artery of God's love. They stand in the way of our being able to accept God's unconditional love for us. They make it tough for us to truly love God, to love ourselves or to love each other. They keep us locked in a prison of bitterness and depression, and make it difficult for God's love to flow through us and out into the world.

For better or worse, many of us project our experience of our father onto our image of God. If that experience has left us with emotional pain, then we are in need of healing. But only we hold the key to that healing, for it can only come about through forgiveness.

Counseling and psychotherapy can help bring these painful memories into our conscious awareness so that we can confront them face to face; so that we can experience and purge ourselves of the anger and the hurt. But for real healing to occur, we ultimately need to forgive; to let go of the bitterness; and to unconditionally forgive our fathers in our hearts. We need to understand that they too were the victims of circumstances, and that given the handicaps they had, they may have done the best they could. To do this, no matter how hard or how long it takes, is to free ourselves for God's healing to take place.

I lost my dad when I was five years old. A victim emotionally wounded by World War II and by life, he spent many years in a Veteran's hospital, and was lobotomized in the late 1950s. I visited him for the first time when I was 15, and came away unaffected, or so I thought. He died a few years later, and I hardly shed a tear for this man whom I really never knew.

In my teens and twenties I successfully kept my feelings about my father buried far away from conscious awareness. I ran; a perfectionist, overachiever, typical Type A personality — run, run, run; do a million things, burn yourself out, just don't let the feelings, don't let the pain get in. It worked. I was very productive. I finished school and built a very good career at a young age; but eventually things fell apart — I couldn't keep running. I found myself very depressed for a long time and didn't know why.

It was in this context that I heard of and visited a priest having the gift of healing. After listening to my story, he asked me to close my eyes. He took me on a journey in my mind to a place where time stood still. He was my guide over the horizon, where Jesus stood beckoning to me.

I left the priest and proceeded to meet Jesus. He hugged me, and told me that he had been waiting with someone who needed to see me. He led me over a bridge to a park bench where my dad was sitting.

Jesus embraced us both, and we embraced each other. He said my dad was sorry; that he needed me to know that he loved me and had tried his best; that he wanted my forgiveness.

I told my dad how much I had missed him and how sorry I was that we hadn't had time together. I told him how much I loved him. I forgave in my heart; forgave this kind and gentle man who truly did not need my forgiveness. In that moment in time, we both were healed.

This experience changed me. It enabled me to open myself more fully to the people in my life; to be a more loving father, a more caring husband. It enabled me to accept the fact that God really did love me — that I was lovable. I believe that it ultimately led me here to be a deacon.

I'd like to share with you this poem that I wrote many years ago, shortly after this experience, in the hope that my healing might be the catalyst for forgiveness and healing wherever it might be needed in your lives.

The Healing

I've had a wish for many years
to put some time aside;
To sit upon an old park bench
with my daddy by my side.

I'd tell him how I missed him.
I'd tell him how I cried.
I'd tell him how I understand
his suffering deep inside.

And then one day it happened
through grace and love you see.
I sat upon that old park bench
with my daddy next to me.

He told me how he loved me.
He told me how he cried.
He asked that I forgive him
for not being by my side.

I told my dad I love him.
I told him that I cared.
I gave him my forgiveness
and a healing we both shared.

Rest, dad. I love you.

May 14, 1985

My sisters and brothers, I wish you a happy and a healing Father's Day.

June 1993
Father's Day

Never Too Late to Go Home

Matthew 20: 1 - 16

(Jesus said), "For the kingdom of heaven is like a landowner who went out early in the morning to hire laborers for his vineyard. When he had agreed with the laborers for a denarius for the day, he sent them into his vineyard. And he went out about the third hour and saw others standing idle in the market place; and to those he said, 'You also go into the vineyard, and whatever is right I will give you.' And so they went. Again he went out about the sixth and the ninth hour, and did the same thing. And about the eleventh hour he went out and found others standing around; and he said to them, 'Why have you been standing here idle all day long?' They said to him, 'Because no one hired us.' He said to them, 'You go into the vineyard too.' When evening came, the owner of the vineyard said to his foreman, 'Call the laborers and pay them their wages, beginning with the last group to the first.' When those hired about the eleventh hour came, each one received a denarius. When those hired first came, they thought that they would receive more; but each of them also received a denarius. When they received it, they grumbled at the landowner, saying, 'These last men have worked only one hour, and you have made them equal to us who have borne the burden and the scorching heat of the day.' But he answered and said to one of them, 'Friend, I am doing you no wrong; did you not agree with me for a denarius? Take what is yours and go, but I wish to give to this last man the same as to you. Is it not lawful for me to do what I wish with what is my own? Or is your eye envious because I am generous?' So the last shall be first, and the first last."

*

If God really loves us unconditionally, then Hell should be an empty place. But if God is truly just, then everyone should ultimately get what's coming to them. So which is it?

God's love and forgiveness for us has no limits — it's unconditional. He loves us when we do good, and when we do not so good. He loves the kind and the mean, the generous and the stingy, the saint and the bigot. Jesus calls us to love and forgive others as God does us, without strings.

Today's Gospel is a parable about God's generosity and how much he really does love us; how he never shuts off that love, never gives up on us; how he patiently stands in the wings as we go through the hours of our life journey, waiting for the moment when we realize he's out there — the moment that we turn to him and love him in return; how, with God, it's never too late. But this Gospel is one of those tough Gospels, like the one about the prodigal son, or about forgiving your neighbor 70 times seven times.

If we tend to be self righteous, it can offend our sense of fairness and justice. How does the worker who punched in five minutes before closing get the same pay as the one who labored all day long? How does the son who squandered away his father's money merit a welcome home party while the son who added to his father's wealth is out working and sweating in the field? How does the thief who was crucified next to Jesus get promised a one way ticket to paradise after living a life of crime?

The underlying question here is how can God be both the just God revealed by Moses in the Old Testament, and at the same time the unconditionally loving and forgiving God revealed by Jesus in these parables? This dichotomy is the mystery of redemption.

Jesus is telling us that God's justice is not our justice. He is using these parables to teach us a great lesson: that God accepts us back from wherever we've been; that he never gives up on us; that with God, it's never too late to go home.

If there really is a geographical place called Hell, I think it must be hard to get there. A person would have to know and feel in the depths of his or her being how very much they were loved by God, and then choose to turn their back and walk away from that love for all eternity. I can't imagine too many people doing that.

God passionately pursues us through the hours of our lives. He waits and waits for the moment that we recognize his love and choose to love him in return.

Maybe if we don't get it right during the work day (the time that we are alive), God meets us at the moment of our death — five minutes before closing, so to speak — and makes us one more offer to still turn to him; an offer we can't refuse.

Maybe heaven is filled with the kinds of people with whom we wouldn't want to associate. Perhaps when we sit down to our first meal in heaven, we will be stunned to see who else is around the table.

Perhaps God's mercy and generosity extends even beyond the tax collectors and the prostitutes, to the bigots, the drug dealers and the worse villains in history. Wouldn't that be a shocker! It would even be worse than seeing those last minute workers in the vineyard getting a full day's pay. But even God couldn't possibly be that loving, that forgiving, that merciful — or could he? And could he really expect you and me to be?

There is a movie I recently saw which deals with this mystery, the mystery of redemption, in a powerful way. It's called *The Bad Lieutenant* and it stars Harvey Keitel in the title role. Though the message of this film is forgiveness and redemption, it contains language and scenes that could be offensive. So, I caution you that both the edited R version and the uncut NC-17 version must be viewed with discretion.

Harvey Keital plays this depraved New York City police Lieutenant. He's on the take; uses and sells the drugs he confiscates on the street; cheats on his wife; and abuses the teenage girls he stops for traffic violations — all in all, a thoroughly corrupt and decadent person. He's a heavy gambler, and into the loan sharks for $120,000 for bets he lost on the World Series. The first hour of the film is used to develop his character as a truly unredeemable human being.

Eventually he is called in to investigate a brutal crime: a young nun is viciously beaten and raped by two teenage hoodlums while she prays alone in church. He presses the nun to reveal the identity of the teenagers, but she will not do so. She knows them well from the local high school, but has only compassion for them, for the poverty and hopelessness in which they were raised. She unconditionally forgives and prays for them, and refuses to assist in their arrest.

It is through this horrible crime that the bad lieutenant finds redemption. Moved by the unconditional love and forgiveness exhibited by the nun, and facing death himself at the hands of the loan sharks whom he has no money to pay, he drinks himself into a stupor and passes out alone in the church.

When he awakes, and reality sets in, he breaks down weeping on the floor in front of the altar. It is here that he encounters Christ, and begs for forgiveness for the bad things he's done in his life. He is comforted by Jesus, and unconditionally forgiven. He is redeemed; and through his redemption he is able to understand and to forgive the teenagers.

Redemption, like so much of the reality of God, is a mystery. But it's God's mystery, not ours.

How can God be both loving and just? The answer is that he doesn't have to be. Love is of God; justice is of the world. If we loved each other the way God calls us to, there would be no need for justice. And if we could feel in the depths of our being, how totally and unconditionally we are loved by God, there would be no need for anyone to ask for our forgiveness.

In this morning's Gospel, Jesus gives us some really good news — with God, it's never too late to go home.

September 1993
Ordinary Time

Passionate Commitment

I noticed something strange this year. Maybe some of you noticed it too. People didn't want to give up Christmas. Driving around New Jersey and even walking down 8th Avenue in midtown Manhattan, I saw that many homes and storefronts still had decorated trees and blinking lights — right into February.

My first reaction towards the middle of January was that people were still exhausted from the Christmas rush; or else too busy to take their decorations down. But as February came and the lights were still blinking on Knickerbocker Road and on 53rd Street, I began to sense that something else might be going on.

Maybe people didn't want to give up Christmas because they were still waiting —waiting for something to fill their longing; to give them peace and happiness; to make them whole; something, or someone, to stretch out a hand and break through the loneliness, the leprosy, and pull them back from inside of themselves. But how could this loneliness happen in such a great and affluent and fun loving society?

Maybe it has to do with the loss of passionate commitment. Our world seems to have abandoned the idea that this wonderful driving force in life is a gift to be cherished. And life can be hollow without passionate commitment; kind of lonely — maybe even like being one of those lepers in today's Gospel.

For commitment to work it has to flow outward, not inward. But the world has moved commitment from the outside to the inside. Instead of promoting commitment to someone or something outside of and more important than ourselves, our modern world glorifies the 'me' in each of us. The world tells us in so many subtle and not so subtle ways that we are *no one* until we achieve self-fulfillment, until we find ourselves and our niche.

But the Gospel tells us that that can never happen while our eyes turn inward. A thousand self-improvement workshops can't fill the longing or remove the loneliness; a library filled with self-help books can't take the place of this Gospel book. And so the waiting goes on — and the Christmas lights still blink.

As people search relentlessly within themselves for that niche, there are casualties. Just like our modern world has perfected the disposable contact lens, it has given us throwaway relationships: friendships, marriages, children, families, jobs — even religions. The mantra of the 70s, 80s and 90s has been: 'If it ain't working, junk it; if you're not happy find someone or someplace or something new.' Who needs commitment anyway? And so, those Christmas lights keep blinking.

But along comes Jesus, 2,000 years ago and every day since. He reaches out into our leprosy, into our loneliness. He tells us about commitment. "Teacher, what is the way to true happiness?" someone asks. *Commit yourself*, Jesus tells him. "Love God with your whole heart and your whole soul and love your neighbor as yourself."

He didn't say lose weight, or win the lottery, or find the perfect job or perfect mate. He said, *commit yourself* — commit yourself, not to yourself, but to God and to others.

We can never find wholeness by turning inside. Wholeness, which is really holiness, comes from passionate commitment — love that flows from within us to our Creator God; to our belief in goodness; to that compassion for others that calls us to action on their behalf; to those relationships in which our lives have unfolded: child to parent, parent to child; friend, lover, sweetheart, spouse.

Jesus calls us forth from our loneliness, and he asks us to commit ourselves to life; not just in a one time sacramental or ceremonial event, but by constantly renewing that commitment, day after day, through good days and bad days, sickness and health, laughter and tears.

One of the greatest gifts of passionate commitment that God has given to us is the gift of marriage. It isn't a coincidence that the Church picked today to celebrate World Marriage Day. It is very fitting that we celebrate the gift of marriage on the eve of Saint Valentine's Day, the day set aside for sweethearts. For marriage is the sacrament for sweethearts who promised to journey through life together — committed to each other for all time.

The Church invites us today to reflect upon that special commitment; and for those of us who are married, to renew that promise with all the passionate commitment in our soul.

In my own life, I am deeply thankful to God for the gift of passionate commitment. To be committed to journey through life as a husband and a father, and to work for God as a deacon are the greatest blessings that I could ever have imagined.

As I walked down 8th Avenue in late January, and I saw those Christmas lights still blinking; as I saw the longing and the waiting in so many faces, I was not walking alone. I was walking hand in hand with my sweetheart, my wife of 26 years, my best friend, Wanda. And as I held her hand I thanked God, as I do each day, for the gift of love and for passionate commitment.

February 1994
World Marriage Day

Home by Another Way

Matthew 2: 1 – 3, 7 – 8, 10 - 12

Now after Jesus was born in Bethlehem of Judea in the days of Herod the king, magi from the east arrived in Jerusalem, saying, "Where is he who has been born King of the Jews? For we saw his star in the east and have come to worship him." When Herod the king heard this, he was troubled . . . Then Herod secretly called the magi and determined from them the exact time the star appeared. And he sent them to Bethlehem and said, "Go and search carefully for the Child; and when you have found him, report to me, so that I too may come and worship him." . . . When they saw the star, they rejoiced exceedingly with great joy. After coming into the house they saw the Child with Mary his mother; and they fell to the ground and worshiped him. Then, opening their treasures, they presented to him gifts of gold, frankincense, and myrrh. And having been warned by God in a dream not to return to Herod, the magi left for their own country by another way.

*

There are certain days as we go through the journey of our life that if we look real carefully over our shoulder we just might catch a glimpse of Herod standing in the road calling to us, asking us to stop by on our way back for a cup of coffee.

This Herod is a pretty clever fellow. He uses charm, confusion, doubt, hurt and anger to get our attention. There are times when Herod's offer looks pretty good. But in the depths of our soul, we know that his intentions are less than noble; that as children of God we must avoid Herod at all costs and go home by another way. We know that for us, like the magi, the only way home is through the manger.

At the moment of our conception, God made a decision that it was time for us to begin our journey. He embraced us like a mother bundles up a beloved child to go out into the cold for the very first time. And just like a parent might slip a little identification note into the child's pocket, just in case he or she should get lost, God put a little piece of himself into each and every one of us. That little piece of God is our immortal soul — it is the Christ-child within us. Life is the journey of our soul back home to its loving creator.

In order to return home to God, we must become whole; and to become whole we ultimately have to recognize and embrace that Christ-child within. We need to become like the wise men and enter the manger. But to do this, we need to leave our baggage at the door because the manger is small — there's only room enough for a loving, trusting heart; a heart that has surrendered control and just wants to be in the presence of that Christ-child. We have to enter the manger on God's terms, not our own — and God's terms sometimes don't make sense to us.

It's hard to be loving and trusting enough to put down our baggage and enter that manger. Herod's voice keeps calling us away. He uses many voices to trick us, like he tried to trick the magi. For some of us he uses the voice of hurt and abandonment as he whispers in our ear, "You can't go in there. What if the Christ-child ends up leaving you or betraying you?" For others he uses the voice of fear and anger, "You can't go in there. What will happen to you if you open yourself and become vulnerable? Won't the Christ-child reject you like so many others have done?" For many he uses the voice of the world, "There will be plenty of time later to enter the manger. Right now you have to get your degree; you have to raise your family; you have to build some security for the future; you have to be a success; you have to find your niche and express yourself."

Herod uses a different voice to keep me out of the manger. It might be the same voice that he tries to use with many of you. It is the voice of frustration and anger at God for appearing to be a passive bystander to the 11:00 o'clock news.

I had begun to prepare this homily late one night in early December. As I sat in my room thinking about the imagery of the manger, my attention was drawn to the TV in the next room. CNN was broadcasting live from a small church in California where a funeral was in progress — a funeral for Polly Klaas, the beautiful twelve year old child abducted at knifepoint by a stranger from a slumber party in her own home. The camera zoomed in on the sanctuary of the church where Polly's family stood crying. As the singer Linda Ronstadt sang Polly's favorite song, *A Whole New World* from *Aladdin*, loving photographs of Polly and her family throughout her brief life were shown on the screen.

I put the draft of my homily down and began to cry. I cried for Polly and her family. And I remembered other children and other families for whom I have wept: Etan Patz, the six year old boy who disappeared twelve years ago on his way to school in Greenwich Village; Yosaf Hawkins, the sixteen year old honor student whose life was taken away by a mob of racists on a Brooklyn street because he, as an African American teenager, had the audacity to visit a friend in their all white neighborhood; Adam Walsh, Sara Anne Wood, Jessica Guzzman, whose mother was a co-worker of mine. The litany could go on and on. In my grief, I felt myself standing at the entrance to the manger wanting to go in for comfort. But Herod came up next to me and whispered in my ear, "Ask him why? Why does he let it keep happening day after day: tragedy, suffering, pain? Why doesn't he do something to stop it? After all, he's in charge, he's God."

As I stood frozen in the doorway of the manger, the gentle eyes of the Christ-child gazed into my soul, and a voice without sound answered me. It is the same voice I have heard many times as I sat alone in the church by the tabernacle. "I have chosen to be small," the voice said, "I do not walk and I do not speak. I need you to be my hands and my feet. I need you to be my voice. I need you and your sisters and brothers to bring my love into the world; to make things different, to be my light in the darkness, my presence in the chaos; to lessen the pain and suffering, to comfort the victims of tragedy until I can bring them and you back home and make everything alright."

To enter the manger, we need to let go of the hurts, the fears and angers. We need to say, "Here I am Lord, I am yours. I trust you. Use me as you see fit to ease the pain in the world. I am yours, I love you, your will be done."

God is always calling us home; but we cannot be distracted by the many voices of Herod. We must go home by another way. The pain and the tragedies that Herod speaks about are very, very real. But, in the end, they will all pass away along with Herod himself, disappearing as if an illusion. The only thing that will remain is the Christ-child within the manger, the note that God slipped into our pocket — the little piece of God within us.

January 1994
Feast of the Epiphany

Difficult People

Luke 24: 13 – 16, 28 – 31, 35

> *And behold, two of them were going that very day to a village named Emmaus, which was about seven miles from Jerusalem . . . While they were talking and discussing, Jesus himself approached and began traveling with them. But their eyes were prevented from recognizing him . . . And they approached the village where they were going, and he acted as though he were going farther. But they urged him, saying, "Stay with us, for it is getting toward evening, and the day is now nearly over." So he went in to stay with them. When he had reclined at the table with them, he took the bread and blessed it, and breaking it, he began giving it to them. Then their eyes were opened and they recognized him; and he vanished from their sight . . . He was recognized by them in the breaking of the bread.*

*

Lately I've been having a tough time spotting Jesus on the road I travel. Instead, I keep running into people who need something from me — attention, sympathy, time, even money. And then there's the short tempered clerk in the store, the person who jumps the line at the bus terminal, and those people who tailgate as I'm trying to pull into my driveway. Jesus must still be hanging out on the road to Emmaus because I haven't seen much of him around here.

I can manage to handle all the above type people. The real cross is dealing with those few difficult people in my life: those loved ones with whom I want to have a close relationship, but whose personalities make it very hard for me to be patient and loving, and who usually manage to bring out the worst in me. Those difficult people I travel with on the road to Emmaus.

But just the other day my eyes were opened a little bit and I think, for a moment, I may have seen Jesus. I was reading a bulletin board at work and noticed a list of lunchtime seminars. One in particular caught my eye: 'Coping with Difficult People'. And as I started to write down the date of the seminar, a realization hit me — I'm a difficult person too.

We all have our personalities. Most of us have debits and credits in this area: traits that are positive and traits that are negative; characteristics that endear us to others and hang-ups that cause us to drive people away. But we are much more than our personalities. The realization of this can help us to forgive and accept the negatives in others — and, eventually, even the negatives in ourselves.

When God sends us into the world, he puts a little piece of himself inside. That little piece of God within each of us is our immortal soul — it is the Christ-child within. My personality is not my soul. It is only the outward manifestation of my environmental conditions and my inherited genetic traits. My personality is the vehicle through which I move through life; through which I travel down the road to Emmaus; through which I can communicate with others. Sometimes that communication is loving and lovable, but sometimes it is angry, bitter and even despicable.

Personality is meant to be utilitarian — to help us get through life. But the object of spiritual life is to transcend the personality; to step away from the limits of time and space, the limits of our wants and needs, the limits of our personality; and to become one with the true Self within — that little piece of God in each of us, the Christ-child within. When we can see past all the debits and credits of the human personality, we can catch a glimpse of the Jesus within. Once our eyes are opened and we can recognize him, it's not so hard to love those difficult people. It's not so hard to even love ourselves.

April 1995
Easter Season

When Caesar and God Collide

Luke 20:21-25

They questioned him, saying, "Teacher, we know that you speak and teach correctly, and you are not partial to any, but teach the way of

God in truth. Is it lawful for us to pay taxes to Caesar, or not?" But he detected their trickery and said to them, "Show me a denarius. Whose likeness and inscription does it have?" They said, "Caesar's." And he said to them, "Then render to Caesar the things that are Caesar's, and to God the things that are God's."

*

Give to Caesar the things that are Caesar's and to God the things that are God's. Into the life of each Christian comes a moment of truth — a moment when Caesar and God collide; when some particular demand of Caesar is perceived by us to be in conflict with the Gospel; a moment when we are called on to make a choice and, if need be, to pay for that choice with a great price.

We are citizens of two worlds. Our first and foremost responsibility is to God — to live and act in accordance with the Gospel. But we also have a responsibility to the lawful authority of the land in which we live. That first responsibility, the one we have to God, is quite clear. Jesus made it simple: we must love God with our whole heart, and love others as we love ourselves. But that other responsibility, the one we have to lawful authority, is not always so clear.

We must constantly weigh our responsibility to Caesar against our responsibility to God. When that which Caesar demands is in conflict with the Gospel, there really is no contest — we must go with God. But sometimes it costs; and that cost can be pretty high.

I'd like to tell you about two people, two of my heroes. They were good Christians and good citizens. Each had a moment of truth; and each chose the Gospel over Caesar.

Saint Thomas Moore was a man for all seasons; a husband, father of four, literary scholar and eminent lawyer. He was also a powerful political administrator in the 16th century as he held the job of Chancellor of England under King Henry VIII. Thomas was an intensely spiritual person who took the Gospel seriously.

King Henry asked him to support his divorce from Catherine of Aragon so that he could marry Anne Boleyn. He also asked that Thomas support separating the English Church from Rome. Thomas chose his responsibility to God over his responsibility to Caesar. He resigned his position as Chancellor. As a consequence, Thomas was ripped away from his family and imprisoned in the Tower of London by the vindictive king. When he refused to reconsider his decision, his estate was confiscated and he was beheaded in front of his family.

Thomas' moment of truth came with a high price tag, not just for him but for his family as well. Yet, he chose the Gospel over Caesar and gave to God the things that are God's.

Viola Liuzzo was someone many of us could relate to. A Detroit housewife and mother of five children in the 1960s. She spent her days chauffeuring her kids back and forth to school, shopping in the supermarket and doing a mountain of endless washes.

One night she was watching the news on TV and saw the evil of segregation and racial injustice. She watched this though the lens of the Gospel. She cradled her five children as she tucked them into bed, and kissed her husband goodbye. With the family station wagon she set out for Montgomery, Alabama to participate in a non-violent civil rights demonstration in defiance of the laws of a racist governor.

Mrs. Liuzzo joined hands with black and white citizens, with priests, rabbis, ministers and nuns to stand up to Caesar. Local members of the Ku Klux Klan shouted obscenities and threatened the lives of the marchers. After the march she volunteered to drive black citizens safely back to their homes in Selma. During one of those rides, a pick-up truck filled with men from the Klan pulled up alongside her station wagon. With a shotgun they took her life.

Viola Liuzzo's moment of truth, like Thomas Moore's, came with a very high price tag indeed, not just for her but for her family as well. Yet she chose the Gospel over Caesar and she gave to God the things that are God's.

While the circumstances of our lives may not be as dramatic, we are, nonetheless, faced with choices between God and Caesar — moments of truth when the demands of our government, our community or our employer are in conflict with the Gospel.

May each of us have the faith and the courage of Thomas Moore and Viola Liuzzo. When we face our own personal moment of truth, may we give to God the things that are his.

July 1995
Ordinary Time

The Man in the Water

Matthew 15:32-38

And Jesus called his disciples to him, and said, "I feel compassion for the people, because they have remained with me now three days and have nothing to eat; and I do not want to send them away hungry, for they might faint on the way." The disciples said to him, "Where would we get so many loaves in this desolate place to satisfy such a large crowd?" And Jesus said to them, "How many loaves do you have?" And they said, "Seven, and a few small fish." And he directed the people to sit down on the ground; and he took the seven loaves and the fish; and giving thanks, he broke them and started giving them to the disciples, and the disciples gave them to the people. And they all ate and were satisfied, and they picked up what was left over of the broken pieces, seven large baskets full. And those who ate were four thousand men, besides women and children.

*

If a homeless man appeared in Washington Square Park and claimed to be the Son of God, what would be the greater proof: if he turned five stale bagels into 2,000 Big Macs, or if he so inspired people to share whatever they had that, for one night throughout New York City, no one went to bed hungry, no one fell asleep without shelter, no one cried from loneliness or despair?

Jesus was filled with love and unconditional acceptance of others. While he walked the hills and shores of Galilee, he called those around him to acts of love and selflessness. He brought out the best in others just by being in his presence.

In today's Gospel, the story of the loaves and the fishes, Jesus worked a wonderful miracle. But what was that miracle? Was it an act of magic that awed the crowd and defied the laws of physical nature? Or was it an act of collective love that defied the laws of human nature?

Was the real miracle in this story not the reproduction of food, but Jesus' ability to get the people in the crowd to share what little food they had; and the discovery that once they opened their hearts and their lunch baskets, there was more than enough food for everyone? Knowing what we do about human nature, the second possibility is the greater miracle.

We all come into the world with a basic human tendency to be self centered and selfish; to put our interests, needs and survival before the love of God and the needs of others; to turn inward rather than reach outward in love with God and with our neighbor.

While our human nature enables us to survive it can also be an obstacle to love. While we focus on ourselves, it is difficult for God's unconditional love to flow through us and out into a troubled world. While we focus on ourselves, it is hard to hear God calling to us in the song of a morning bird or the patter of a summer night's rain; to see God in the eyes of our children, in the smile of our lover; in the companionship of a colleague or a co-worker. While we focus on ourselves, it is difficult to hear the cries of the lonely, the desperation of the oppressed, and the hunger of the poor. While we focus on ourselves, not only do we miss the chance to love and to reach out to others, but we run the risk of becoming so self-absorbed that we, like Narcissus, drown in our own reflection.

But while we all possess this basic human tendency to be self-centered, there is a light that shines within our souls that continuously calls us to break out of the prison of selfishness. This light is Christ present within every human being — whether we recognize this presence or not; whether we are Christian, Jewish, Muslim, Buddhist, Hindu, Taoist, agnostic or atheist. And the Christ within calls each of us forth like Lazarus from the tomb, to emerge from our prison of self-centeredness with acts of service and heroic love for our sisters and brothers. Each time we answer 'yes' to this call a miracle happens.

I have witnessed many miracles in my life. I have seen children and adults carry food and clothing into the park on freezing winter mornings to comfort the homeless. I have seen a frail young woman, shivering in the snow, hand back a blanket and tell us about a man sleeping in a cardboard box on the next street who was sick and needed it more. I have seen students spend their spring break building homes for the poor and tutoring inner city children. I have seen administrators and faculty comforting the victims of tragedy. I have seen successful and powerful executives share their stories about struggling with addictions and mental illness to help encourage others who were locked in similar prisons.

These are the real miracles that Jesus brings about — not parlor tricks, but calling out the best in each of us; helping us to defy the laws of self-interest and survival to take care of others.

One of the most moving miracles that I ever heard about happened back in December of 1981 when an Air Florida jet tragically crashed into the Potomac River during an aborted takeoff from Washington DC. I remember reading this story in the *New York Times* and being moved to tears:

HERO OF 737 DISASTER VANISHED UNDER RIVER

An unidentified passenger helped others to safety before vanishing in the icy waters of the Potomac after the Air Florida crash here Wednesday. The passenger was bald, about 50 years old, one of half a dozen survivors clinging to wreckage bobbing in the river when the first rescue helicopter arrived. Life vests were dropped. The man passed them to the others. On two occasions he handed away a lifeline from the hovering helicopter that could have pulled him to safety. 'That guy was amazing' said a paramedic aboard the helicopter. 'All I can tell you is I've never seen that kind of guts. It seemed like he decided that the women and the men who were bleeding needed to get out before him and even as he was going under he stuck to his decision and helped them all get out. My partner and I were talking as we went back over' continued the paramedic, 'that even if he was under and we could see him we were going to get him out. Man that was bravery.' But there was no trace of the man whose identity could not be learned.

I have often wondered about that man in the water. Who was he? What was he? Was he a saint or a sinner before the crash? Loving husband or adulterer? Did he spend his time helping out in soup kitchens or embezzling funds from clients? Did he go to church or temple or did he never pray? Whoever and whatever he was before the crash, on that day in December he was called by God to perform a miracle and he said, 'yes'.

My sisters and brothers let us thank God for miracles, for the loaves and the fishes, and for the man in the water.

March 1996
Lent

Seventy Times Seven

Matthew 18: 21 – 22

Then Peter came and said to him, "Lord, how often shall my brother sin against me and I forgive him? Up to seven times?" Jesus said to him, "I do not say to you, up to seven times, but up to seventy times seven."

*

Jesus says that when someone hurts us we must forgive that someone seventy times seven times. By using the image, Jesus is really saying that there is to be no limits or strings to our forgiving someone and allowing them back into our heart. In 1956, Dag Hammarskjold, who was then Secretary General of the U.N., commenting on the meaning of this kind of forgiveness said, "Forgiveness is the answer to a child's dream of a miracle by which what is broken is made whole again, what is soiled is again made clean."

Jesus is telling us through Peter that the greatest gift we can give to another person, and to ourselves, is the gift of forgiveness. Forgiveness is the act of letting go of the past and accepting someone back into our heart; of extending our hand and allowing ourselves once more to be vulnerable to another. When Jesus tells Peter that we must forgive someone seventy times seven times, he is really telling us that we must forgive unconditionally; that there can be no bounds, no strings, no limits to the amount of times we let someone back into our heart.

To genuinely forgive someone in the way that Jesus speaks about we must be willing to accept the reality that a person's faults and personality quirks will probably not disappear overnight. Jesus asks us to forgive even when the person who hurt us is not sorry; or even when we know that despite someone's sincere apology, they are likely to hurt us again. He asks us to look into the eyes of someone who has hurt us deeply and to show that someone love and acceptance instead of anger and rejection. It is a great gift of unconditional love when we once again open ourselves to trust someone who has really hurt us and let us down.

The kind of forgiveness Jesus asks us to give as a gift to another is really a gift to ourselves as well. It frees us to admit to ourselves that we do not have the knowledge or the wisdom to sit as judge, jury and executioner over someone who has hurt us. To forgive seventy times seven times is a choice that God gives us. We choose life, and love and a relationship for ourselves and for others when we choose to forgive. We relieve ourselves of the burden of carrying around hurt, pain and anger. And we give someone else the freedom to live his or her life — or maybe to rest in peace — with the knowledge that they are loved without strings.

When we forgive, we are not only offering unconditional love but we are taking responsibility for our own lives. We no longer sit and wait for someone else to change for us to be happy; instead we choose to change our own reaction. By so doing, we are opening the door for true healing to occur — healing within ourselves; healing within another; and healing of a relationship.

An example of this kind of healing is in the story of a young man named Kevin who was a colleague of mine several years ago. Kevin shared with me how he had hated his father. He told me how all he ever wanted was for his dad to hold him, say he loved him and tell him that he was proud of his accomplishments. But Kevin's dad was never able to show him this kind of affection.

In high school, if Kevin brought home a B+ average, his father belittled him for not getting an A. In college Kevin didn't graduate high enough in his class. When Kevin fell in love and married outside of his religion, his father stopped speaking to him and forbade him to visit. Eventually Kevin's hurt became so heavy that he had a breakdown and was hospitalized for a while with depression.

But little by little, Kevin's spirit began to heal as he found the gift of forgiveness and freely gave it away without strings. Kevin learned to forgive himself for not being the perfect person his father had wanted. Once he did that, he was able to forgive his father and to accept him for the person he was without expecting him to change.

One day I was having lunch with Kevin and he smiled and told me that he had been in his dad's arms 28 times over the past few months. When I asked if his dad had finally started hugging him, Kevin said, 'no'. He told me that he had started hugging his father and had learned that it doesn't really matter who starts a hug.

Kevin had come to a point of healing and wholeness. He had come to forgive without strings; and in so doing was making the connection with his dad that he so very much had wanted for many years.

Kevin's story represents what Jesus speaks about when he tells us to forgive seventy times seven times. Jesus tells us to plant our own garden instead of sitting around and waiting for someone else to send us flowers.

This kind of unconditional forgiveness is its own reward. It is the answer to a child's dream of a miracle — a miracle by which what is broken is made whole again, and what is soiled is again made clean.

August 1996
Ordinary Time

Miracles

Miracles aren't always what we expect them to be. Miracles are happening everyday all around us; miracles are happening everyday within us.

*

Fox was a 45 year old homeless man who lived for nine years at the George Washington Bridge Bus Terminal. He had lost a leg many years ago, and survived by spinning his wheelchair in and out of traffic and up and down subway ramps begging. One morning, I was bringing coffee and sandwiches to homeless people living in cardboard boxes near the terminal. I tapped the shoulder of a man who was bundled up asleep in blankets in a big cardboard box and asked if he would like some coffee. He thanked me and took the coffee. I asked his name and he said, "Fox." Two weeks later I was bringing breakfast to the same place and saw him again. He was sleeping; and I gently woke him by calling his name, "Fox, Fox." He awoke and smiled and said in amazement, "You remembered my name."

Over the years Fox had become a dear friend to my wife and me, our children and to many members of our parish Outreach Team. We would see him often as we distributed food and clothing to the homeless people in upper Manhattan. I would see him almost every morning as I went to work, and often brought him sandwiches from home. Sometimes, after a hard day at work, I would drag myself up the subway ramp and he would see me and tell me that he was worried about me because I looked so tired. This man who had nothing was worried about me who had so much.

One day I learned that Fox had died in the streets near the terminal of an apparent drug overdose. With the help of the NYPD detectives, I was able to locate Fox's body at the City Morgue where it had been for a month, an unidentified casualty of the streets. With the kindness of our local funeral parlor and the generosity of the priests in my parish, I was able to bring Fox's body to Tenafly to be buried with dignity by the many friends who loved him.

A memorial Mass was celebrated at Our Lady of Mount Carmel and 35 of his friends — children and adults — were present. He was then buried in Mount Carmel Cemetery. An Episcopal Church near the Bus Terminal permitted me to hold a special memorial service for Fox and to invite all the homeless men and women who knew him.

At the service, one of Fox's friends shared an emotional eulogy. He told us how 'Brother Fox' had given his friends courage and inspiration to take responsibility for building a better life for themselves; how he had been a loving, caring friend; and how much his friends had loved him.

Several months after Fox's death, I had an incredible dream. In it, I was walking in a beautiful sunlit meadow. I heard someone calling my name and in the distance I saw Fox waving to me from his wheelchair. He had a blanket over his lap. As I got closer I heard him shouting, "Lex, Lex, come here. I got something I want to show you!" Fox pulled the blanket off his lap, stood up and danced around with joy. He had two legs and he was whole. I woke up with the most wonderful, peaceful, joyful feeling I have ever experienced.

I believe Fox really came to me in that dream to give me a gift. It was the gift of showing me how much he was loved by God. That despite the circumstances of his death God had healed Fox, made him whole, and welcomed him home. It was Fox's way of telling me that everything I believe is really true. That in the end God finds a way, despite the circumstances of our death, to heal us and make us whole.

I believe that our loving Father in heaven heals us and makes us whole in ways beyond our human understanding — beyond our human concepts of justice and salvation. I believe that no human soul is ever lost; that God finds a way to heal and make whole each and every one of his children regardless of the most tragic circumstances.

Be at peace if there is someone in your life who left this world because of a painful illness or under tragic circumstances, even the tragedy of murder or suicide. For even in the darkest moment,   God touches us and makes us whole.

The   Good Shepherd will never give up until he can cradle and comfort each and every one of his sheep — even those we may think of as lost — in his arms.

Miracles aren't always what we expect them to be. Miracles are happening everyday all around us; miracles are happening everyday within us.

February 1997
Ordinary Time

The Holy Family

One of my favorite gospels is the story about the Prodigal Son. Remember that one? The teenager cannot stand to stay another day with his family. He asks his father for his inheritance ahead of schedule, and goes off to squanders every last penny on wine, women and song. He hits rock bottom and comes crawling home to beg his dad for a job as a laborer in the family business. The best part of the story is how the father jumps up and down for joy when he sees his son approaching the house and runs out to embrace him and welcome him home.

This story, for me, embodies the core of Jesus' message to us: unconditional love, unconditional forgiveness. Jesus teaches us to never shut the door of our heart to another person. Jesus teaches us to never let a relationship wither and die.

Now, you'd probably find a few 20th century psychotherapists who would look at the story of the father and his Prodigal Son and yell, 'codependency!' Who would label the relationship as dysfunctional and call the father an enabler. Yet Jesus holds this relationship up to us as the model of how we are to love and forgive each other.

Today is the feast day of the Holy Family, the day that we celebrate Jesus, Mary and Joseph. We look at Jesus and his mom and dad and see in them the perfect family. But each and every human family, including yours and mine, is called to be a holy family.

Yet how many of us grieve over failed relationships in our own families. How many of us have closed an emotional door on a hopeless relationship, one that has caused us pain; one in which we have been hurt or have inflicted hurt.

A relationship may have died, a door slammed shut. A family that had the potential for wholeness, a holy family, may have been aborted. And in place of that potential holy family stands grieving, alienated, lonely individuals.

My sisters and brothers, perhaps on this feast of the Holy Family, perhaps in this season of Christmas, we can begin to unlock those emotional doors once again.

Perhaps we can take the first step and reach out across the years, across the miles to heal relationships that have been broken. Perhaps with the grace of our loving God in our hearts, we can change dysfunction into holiness.

January 1999
Feast of the Holy Family

Teach Them Well

John Henry Newman was an English Cardinal who died in 1890 at the age of 89. He began his life work as an Anglican priest and scholar; converted to Roman Catholicism in 1845; was ordained a Catholic priest, eventually a bishop and later named a Cardinal by the pope. Cardinal Newman was a deeply spiritual and joyful human being. He saw and celebrated the holiness of what we do in our everyday life: of how close we walk with God when we lovingly and consistently fulfill the duties associated with the many roles we play in the world; of how much we bring God into the world through simple acts of love, friendship and personal influence; of how often we attain sainthood not so much by our words but by our everyday actions.

Cardinal Newman left us a beautiful prayer that I try to read and reflect on each day:

> *God has created me to do Him some definite service. He has committed some work to me which He has not committed to another. I have my mission — I may never know it in this life, but I shall be told it in the next. I am a link in a chain, a bond of connection between persons. He has not created me for naught. I shall do good, I shall do His work; I shall be a preacher of truth in my own place, while not intending it, if I do but keep His commandments and serve Him in my calling.*

God sent each of us into the world with a mission, a calling. As our lives unfold, we find ourselves in a garden — a garden we can call 'our circumstances in life.' It is a garden unique to our own individual calling, our own personal life story. Our garden is the everyday ordinary time of our life. But in that ordinary time is our mission, our reason for being.

And in our garden there are beautiful flowers. But instead of being called roses and tulips and orchids, our flowers are called children and spouses, friends and co-workers, students, patients, clients, parishioners — the list goes on and on. In the end, life isn't about being the most successful or renowned person in our profession or field of endeavor. It's about caring for and loving those flowers.

Today is Father's Day and I'd like to reflect on the garden of parenthood. I could say exactly the same things were it Mother's Day because what I have to say applies equally to mothers and fathers alike. It's about the mission, the calling, the vocation of being a parent.

When I baptize a child, I always tell the mom and dad that the greatest work they will ever do is to teach their child about God. And they will teach their children the *reality* of God not with words, not with books, not even by raising them in the Church. They will teach their children what God really is by loving them unconditionally. Just like Cardinal Newman said — not by words but by actions.

The Gospel tells us that God is love. Everything else we attribute to God is a semantic analogy — a metaphor to help our limited human minds grasp this reality: God is love. When a little child is loved that way, he or she knows in the depths of every cell of his or her being what love is — what God is. And by receiving that love, that child will walk through life with God close by his or her side — even though it may, at times, be in ways that we find hard to understand; even though it may be outside of the Church we love so dearly. And by receiving that love, that child in turn will teach his or her own children about God — that God is love; not by words but by actions.

For those of us who have been called to be fathers and mothers, this very ordinary mission, this everyday job, is the greatest work that we will ever do. We may also be doctors, gas station attendants, lawyers, teachers and clerks, but the work of being a loving parent is our primary mission. It will have the most far reaching effects because if we do that work well, if we carry out the mission that God has given us to the fullest, our children will know God in their hearts; and that intimacy will be carried with them into the relationships that they will have during their own life journeys.

This Father's Day let us — fathers and mothers alike — see and celebrate the holiness of what we do in our everyday life; of how closely we walk with God; how much we are like our Father in heaven, when we unconditionally and consistently love and forgive and remain present to our children — the flowers that God has planted in the garden of our lives.

June 1999
Father's Day

Spirituality is Being in Love with God

Somewhere along my journey I heard this old Christian fable: This parishioner is walking down the road that leads into Rome hoping to visit all the churches in the Holy City. In the distance he sees an angel leaving Rome at a very fast pace. The angel rushes past him carrying a burning torch in one hand and a bucket of water in the other. The parishioner calls out to the angel, "Angel, where are you going in such a hurry?" The angel stops, turns to the parishioner and says, "I'm off to burn down all the mansions in heaven and put out all the fires in hell, and then we'll see who really loves God!"

*

I think it's safe to say that all of us here at Mass today are religious. But how many of us are spiritual? Religion by itself is a tool, a vehicle, very much like a language. It helps us to communicate our understanding of God, of life and death and of our own mortality. Using the structure of religion, we communicate our understanding of these mysteries both horizontally to others in our own time and vertically to future generations of history.

Spirituality, on the other hand, blossoms out of and transcends religion. It is the non verbal essence of that unique and intimate relationship between each one of us and God. Spirituality is being in love with God.

The difference between being just religious and being religious <u>and</u> spiritual is like the difference between being a married couple who just live together for a lifetime and being a married couple who live together and remain passionately in love with each other for a lifetime. A couple can live together in marriage for decades without passion, without being in love. And that would be very sad. That marriage would be like a body without a heart. Likewise, a person can be very religious; can practice every devotion known to the Church; can spend the day talking only about God. But if this devotion is done without feeling the presence of God as an intimate and personal friend, it is like a marriage without passion.

Psalm 16 is a beautiful expression of spirituality, of the soul in love with God:

> *I said to the Lord, "You are my Lord;*
> *I have no good besides You . . .*
> *You will make known to me the path of life;*
> *In Your presence is fullness of joy;*
> *In Your right hand there are pleasures forever."*
>
> Psalm 16: 2, 11

We are spiritual when our heart is totally open to God's love; when we feel God so present in our life that we want to love him back in the same unconditional way. And we try to love all his other children as he loves us.

Spirituality doesn't know from mansions in heaven or fires in hell. Spirituality isn't a quid pro quo. It's not about leading a good life so that we make it into heaven. It's about leading a good life because we are so filled with God's love for us that there is no other way we could possibly live.

Spirituality is being in love with God. When we are in love with God, we are already in heaven. When we turn ourselves away from God, we are in hell. Either way, the choice is ours and the time is now. There is only this moment, the reality of God's love and his invitation to each of us to return that love.

So if you see an angel carrying a torch and a bucket of water, smile and be assured that after those mansions are all burnt down and those fires quenched, your soul will remain with abounding joy basking in the glow of God's love forever.

September 1999
Ordinary Time

The Gospel of You

Mark 12: 28-30

One of the scribes came and heard them arguing, and recognizing that (Jesus) had answered them well, asked him, "What commandment is the foremost of all?" Jesus answered, "The foremost is, 'Hear, O Israel! The Lord our God is one Lord; and you shall love the Lord your God with all your heart, and with all your soul, and with all your mind, and with all your strength.' The second is this, 'You shall love your neighbor as yourself.' There is no other commandment greater than these."

*

Officially the Church recognizes only four Gospels: Matthew, Mark, Luke and John; but in reality there are many, many gospels. Just in this room alone there are over 200 gospels in the making. One of my teachers in formation for the diaconate made a point that has stayed with me: each of us is writing a gospel, little by little, day by day. It is the gospel of you; the gospel of me — for each of our lives is a gospel. And by writing this gospel we are telling the world about Jesus of Nazareth; and in the process, we are slowly growing into the people that we will be for all eternity. In the end our gospel can be truly beautiful, but how it turns out depends on our understanding of who Jesus really is, and how we translate that understanding into the way we subsequently interact with others and live out our lives.

It's not so easy to understand who Jesus really is; lots of things can get in the way: our fears, our prejudice, our tendency to label and to exclude people who are different from us; and the presence of anger in our hearts. These obstacles can keep Jesus a stranger.

Even the disciples who lived day after day with Jesus didn't get it right away. It took time and a series of incremental moments of enlightenment to slowly open their eyes. Through their encounters with the resurrected Jesus and the subsequent transformation that occurred within them on Pentecost, the disciples, little by little, came to understand Jesus.

Their enlightenment unfolded in the choices that they made and the way they lived out the rest of their lives. Each one of those lives was in fact a gospel, because through those lives the world experienced the healing presence of God. It has continued to happen down through the centuries. And it still happens today. Through the unconditional love and acceptance of others that is demonstrated by modern day disciples, the world continues to experience Jesus in its midst. But this can't happen until our eyes our open and we understand what Jesus wants of us.

It is hard for many of us to understand and accept what Jesus is asking. We hear the story where Jesus was asked by someone what the most important commandment is; and his answer that it is to love God with our whole heart. But we can easily overlook the rest of his answer, the part where he says that the second commandment is just as important — to love each other the way we love ourselves. Love, not hate. Love, not bigotry. Love, not anger or revenge. What kind of a gospel are we writing with our lives?

Jesus was about love. It is hard for me to imagine a Jesus who went year after year without speaking to a brother or a sister, a parent or a child, or a friend because of some hurt or some unacceptable behavior. How about a Jesus who voted for the death penalty, or one who got upset that more tax dollars were being spent on poor school children than on those of the affluent. What kind of a gospel are we writing?

It is hard for me to imagine a Jesus who would exclude anyone from his friendship because he or she was gay; or who separated his friends along racial, economic or gender boundaries.

When we look around, when we read the papers or watch the news, we can see how many people do not know Jesus. The world is in great need of unconditional love, of unconditional acceptance — the kind of healing that Jesus was all about. The world is hungry for the story, just as it was 2,000 years ago. That story, that gospel, can reach out through you and through me. We are writing a gospel little by little, day by day.

What kind of a gospel is it?

February 1999
Ordinary Time

A parent speaks to a child in analogies and metaphors that the child's mind can comprehend. These analogies and metaphors get adjusted from the most simple, when the child is an infant, to real life *'that's how it really is'* facts when the child is an adult.

The parent always speaks truth but that truth is presented in a language that, given the intellectual and social development of the child, he or she is capable of grasping.

I think that God speaks to humanity through his revelation in a similar way that a parent speaks to and teaches a child. God uses analogies and metaphors and reveals them through the lens of a particular historical moment in humanity's intellectual development; and, further, through the prism of a given culture which, by the way, is also in progressive stages of intellectual development.

Thus the stories of Creation, Adam and Eve or Abraham, for example: did God really make the world in six days; did our first parents really blow it for all of us and bring death, suffering and pain into our lives by eating an apple, or is God revealing his truth to us through an analogy and at a particular time in human development (3,000 to 5,000 years ago); did Abraham really almost murder his beloved son to please God or, is God, again, making a point with an analogy that a culture that was surrounded by pagan sacrifice of first born sons to Baal can mentally grasp.

This does not discount that God revealed truth and inspired the writers whom he used as vehicles for recording that truth. But it tells us that God continues to reveal the same truth in progressive stages of history and culture, when humanity's intellectual development reaches another level of comprehension.

So, when science presents the biological and anthropological picture of plants, animals and humans evolving over billions of years, this is really not in conflict with our faith. The fact is that our loving God did in fact create us to know, love and serve him. How that fact gets across to us is dependent upon how much we are able to grasp at the time. Could Moses or Isaiah have begun to understand a biological process that unfolded over billions of years at a time when mankind believed that the sky was a canopy with holes cut into it for light and water to get through?

If archeologists find some physical proof that Moses really didn't part the Red Sea in two, but that such a thick fog settled over the beach between the Israelites and Pharaoh's army that Moses and his people were able to escape, that doesn't diminish the truth that God did indeed bring the Israelite's out of bondage.

And if we found out some day that Jesus didn't use magic to multiply a few loaves of bread and fishes to feed a multitude of people, but that his goodness and love inspired people in the crowd to generously share the food that they were hoarding, it in no way diminishes who Jesus is and what his redemptive mission on earth was all about.

During this Lenten season let us reflect on the essence of our Catholic faith. That essence is timeless and limitless and unchanging. As we intellectually evolve through human history and culture and are able — through advances in science, biblical scholarship and medicine — to experience more of God's universe, let our faith and our hearts and our minds not be troubled. In the words of Saint Teresa of Avila, a great doctor of the church, "*all things are passing God only is changeless.*"

February 2002
Carmel Retreat House

Hungry No More

John 6: 35

Jesus said to them, "I am the bread of life; he who comes to me will not hunger, and he who believes in me will never thirst."

*

"Whoever comes to me will never hunger." For I am with you in the chaos and the darkness. I am present in the pain, the loss, the suffering. I am there at the center of the contradiction; at the center of the cross. "I am the Bread of life."

I get pretty hungry when I watch TV. It may have something to do with what I watch. I'm hooked on CNN and Eyewitness News. Thanks to television news I get to be a witness to history — a bystander to reality; a fly on the wall of life.

Thanks to television news, I am there live — at the center of the chaos; at the center of the contradiction: from ethnic cleansing in Bosnia to the murders of Ronald Goldman and Nicole Brown Simpson; from genocide in Rwanda to massacre on the Long Island railroad; from the World Trade Center bombing to the kidnapping of a 12 year old child in California — right there in the middle of the chaos, and it makes me pretty hungry. But it's the kind of hunger that just won't go away, no matter how much junk food I stuff into my mouth as I watch the television screen. It's a hunger for an answer to the contradiction of life — why does God permit all this evil and suffering to exist?

I get pretty hungry as I commute to work in the city each morning. I get a first hand view into reality on every subway car I ride; every street corner I pass. From the pretty young woman who sells her body to get money for crack; to the homeless young alcoholic from Cresskill who lives in the subway; from the drug dealers who work bankers hours outside of the NYU dorms; to the schizophrenic lady who raves at the squirrels in Washington Square Park — I am right there in the middle of the chaos and it makes me pretty hungry. But it's the kind of hunger that just won't go away no matter how many bagels I eat, or cups of coffee I drink once I get to my office. It's a hunger for an answer to the contradiction of life — why is there all this pain and suffering in the world?

I even get hungry sometimes when I come here to church. I look out into your faces — the faces of my sisters and brothers, my friends with whom I share the journey of faith — and I know many of your stories. There are some of you who are lonely; others struggle with physical, emotional and spiritual pain; unemployment; or the loss of a loved one. There are families who have lost a child through sickness or tragedy; and children who have lost a parent through illness or a sudden and untimely death. And sometimes, even here in the comfort of my faith and with the brother and sisterhood of our Christian community, sometimes even here I get hungry. And I ask God, *why?*

But in these moments of confusion and hunger, I can hear Jesus calling to me in the Gospel, *Come to me if you are hungry. I am the bread of life, the answer to the contradiction.*

And as my eyes come to gaze upon the cross, I begin to understand. No matter how hard we try, no one of us can escape the pain and contradictions of human existence. The symbol of our faith is itself a contradiction: the cross, two opposing beams of wood made from the tree of life, used to torture and destroy life; and in the center of the contradiction, we have God in human form.

But the message of the cross is hope. It tells us that we are not alone; that God is with us in the chaos and the darkness; he is present in the pain, the loss, the suffering; he is there at the center of the contradiction, at the center of our cross. And someday, once we are free of the constraints of human existence and the limitations of human understanding, it will all make sense; there will be a happy ending — or rather, a happy beginning. As we are embraced by our loving Father and are reunited with our loved ones, there will be no more pain, no more suffering, no more hunger.

And as I pray before the cross, a voice from deep within the center of my soul answers all my questions, and gives me the nourishment I need to go on with my journey:

> *I am with you in the chaos and the darkness,*
> *I am present in the pain, the loss, the suffering,*
> *I am there at the center of the contradiction,*
> *at the center of the cross.*
> *I am the Bread of life.*

July 1994
Ordinary Time

The Christmas Moment

Luke 1: 30 – 31, 34 – 35, 36

The angel said to her, "Do not be afraid, Mary . . . behold, you will conceive in your womb and bear a son, and you shall name him Jesus . . ." Mary said to the angel, "How can this be, since I am a virgin?" The angel answered and said to her, "The Holy Spirit will come upon you, and the power of the Most High will overshadow you . . ." And Mary said, "(Behold the handmaid of the Lord) . . . may it be done to me according to your word."

*

Just like that little stable in Bethlehem 2,000 years ago, there is a Christ-child within each of us. It is our immortal soul, our true Self. It is that little piece of God that our loving Creator put inside us at the moment of our conception. Sometimes a person can search a whole lifetime, looking for what was inside right from the start.

Like baby Jesus in the stable was wrapped in swaddling clothes, our Christ-child is wrapped too. But instead of swaddling clothes, he is wrapped in layers and layers of personality and lifetime experience — personal history that over time can hide and obscure the real Christ within us.

Those layers seem to take on an identity of their own as our personality develops. We give them a name: I, Ego, Lex, Mary, John, Ashley, etc. But the I, the Ego is not the true Self. Just like those swaddling clothes, our personality is a temporary garment. The real Christ-child is inside — inside each of us.

By God's grace there will be a Christmas moment in each of our lives: a moment of unwrapping those garments, discarding those soiled layers and layers of personal history; a moment of recognizing and embracing the Christ within us. The saints, those holy men and holy women, came to that Christmas moment and lived the rest of their days as a reflection of the Christ they found within. For most people the road to that stable is a lifetime journey. But each one of us is called to that Christmas moment.

We get distracted by the world. Sometimes we are overwhelmed by our fears, our anxieties, and our depression. As we get more and more wrapped up in our own ego, our own needs and wants, it is harder to see that little Christ-child within. The way to find that Child, the way to holiness and true mental health, is to reach outside of ourselves; to let go of our own needs and wants, our hurts and disappointments, our anger, and to make our hearts totally open to God.

We have an excellent example of how to do this. The Church has always taught us that Mary is a role model, an archetype for how we should live our lives. Mary let go of her fears and confusion and made herself a vessel of God. When she said to the angel, "May it be done to me according to your word," she gave herself totally away to God, and in so doing, she found herself. That was Mary's Christmas moment. Many months before she actually entered that stable in Bethlehem, Mary entered the stable of her heart, unwrapped the layers of her own will and embraced the Christ within her.

Each one of us is called to our own personal Christmas moment; to follow Mary's example; to give ourselves away to God — to enter our own stable and find the presence of God within us, our true Self, for all eternity.

December 1996
Advent

Becoming a Father for Others

"Our Father who art in heaven, hallowed be thy name." Jesus gave us a wonderful gift: he brought God into the center of our lives and taught us that he was like a loving father. Today is Father's Day. It is a good time to remember that each and every one of us — male and female alike — is called to mirror the fatherhood of God in our relationships with others.

*

It is a great joy for me as a deacon to baptize a child. The joy of administering the sacrament as an ordained minister of the Church is for me magnified by the fact that I am a father myself. I have been given the blessing of raising four wonderful children; and I know — first hand — the joys and responsibilities of being a father.

The greatest responsibility of a parental father is to mirror the unconditional love of our heavenly Father. Fathers have been given a very special mission in life: they are called to teach their children that God is unconditional love. And they do this teaching — they carry out this mission — not with books, not even necessarily with words. They do it by example — by loving their child, unconditionally, without strings, no matter what.

God loves each and every one of us in a personal and unconditional way. The seed of that love is inside of us all. And that seed is watered to grow into a beautiful flower by the unconditional love we receive from our parents.

But that flower can still grow even in the absence of parental love, even in the presence of abuse, of abandonment, of neglect; because that seed is innately watered by God's grace. And that flower can still grow even in the harshest conditions, by our experience of the Gospel, by the sacraments and by the love of other people.

That flower blooms in our lives when we make the transition from receiver to giver. When we say 'yes' to the presence of God's love in our life and share that love with others — when we live the Gospel.

I have known people who have suffered greatly because they did not experience the love of a parental father. But I believe we have a choice: we can spend decades in depression over what we missed as a child, or we can cross over the bridge, make the transition from receiver to giver and become a father for others.

We can become a father for others not only in a parental way. We can be a father to our children, but we can also be a father to our workers, our students, our parishioners, our friends — to all those with whom we interact. This type of father is neither male nor female; it is the bearer of unconditional love — it is the mirror of our heavenly Father.

God's love comes to fruition in our lives when we generously let it flow through us to others. So this Father's Day let us thank our heavenly Father for our blessings. Let us reach out to our parental fathers, living and deceased, with love and gratitude, with compassion, and if need be, with forgiveness. And let us make *Our Father* who art in heaven visible here on earth through the unconditional fatherly love that we generously share with others.

June 1998
Father's Day

The Idealized Holy Family

Luke 2: 41 – 48, 52

Now his parents went to Jerusalem every year at the Feast of the Passover. And when he became twelve, they went up there according to the custom of the Feast; and as they were returning, after spending the full number of days, the boy Jesus stayed behind in Jerusalem. But his parents were unaware of it, but supposed him to be in the caravan, and went a day's journey; and they began looking for him among their relatives and acquaintances. When they did not find him, they returned to Jerusalem looking for him. Then, after three days they found him in the temple, sitting in the midst of the teachers . . . When they saw him, they were astonished; and his mother said to him, "Son, why have you treated us this way? Behold, your father and I have been anxiously looking for you." . . . And he went down with them and came to Nazareth, and he continued in subjection to them; and his mother treasured all these things in her heart.

*

I like the saints, all of them. But, something we tend to forget about the saints is that they were human beings. They weren't perfect. They had good days and bad days like each of us. And we especially like to idealize the Holy Family as being perfect: the epitome of peace and calmness; the pinnacle of human family interaction without an ounce of dysfunction.

We put them on a pedestal as role models, making it impossible for us and our families to ever measure up. And something we tend to overlook about Jesus: even though he was the son of God, he was also fully human.

But today's Gospel shows that they were flesh and blood like us. They faced real problems and had moments of anxiety and even dysfunction just like you and me. And that doesn't negate their holiness. Quite the opposite: it makes them real role models; because in those moments of anxiety and dysfunction, they never gave up. They kept responding to God's love and doing their best to be loving and to follow his will. And that is all that any one of us is called to do.

In the Gospel story, Jesus is a 12 year old teenager who wanders off while the family is returning from their annual vacation in Jerusalem. He was gone for a day before his parents realized that he was missing. And when they did they panicked and went running through the caravan looking for him for three more days. If they had had the technology that we have, Jesus' picture would have been on milk containers, an amber alert would have gone off, and John Walsh would be on the case.

When they find him they ask why he did such a terrible thing to them, "Son, why have you done this to us? Your father and I have been looking for you with great anxiety."

Jesus sort of brushes it off and tells them they should have known better; that he was out doing God's work. Like I said, he was a teenager.

Joseph and Mary must have read him the riot act because he goes back with them, and doesn't leave home again for 18 years.

So what's the lesson here?

The holy family was truly human, and yet it was also truly holy.

We need to look to Mary and Joseph and all the saints, not as plaster or wooden statues, not as idealized examples of unattainable perfection, but as flesh and blood human beings just like us.

We are all called to be holy, despite the drama, anxiety and dysfunction that we sometimes find ourselves and our families mired in; despite the mistakes we inevitably make.

We are all called to be saints. We don't have to be perfect. We just have to never stop loving. We just have to never give up.

December 2009
Feast of the Holy Family

We Are Loved

I recently took a day off from work and was home alone in the house for a while. I picked up this magazine, *U.S. Catholic*, and happened on an article that caught my eye — *The Seven Secrets of Successful Catholics*. Now I'm embarrassed to tell you that a title like this will usually turn me off. I make unfair generalizations that this kind of a title usually indicates an author who believes that only Catholics have a lock on salvation.

Despite my prejudice, I began to read and found the article and the author to be filled with loving spirituality. But when I got to Secret Number Six I found myself crying. Here I was alone in the house, except for the two cats, and crying. But these were no ordinary tears: they were tears of joy because what I had read in Secret Number Six resonated with something deep within my soul.

Secret Number Six stated that, "Successful Catholics always remember that God is merciful and forgiving." The article went deeper: "Successful Catholics recognize all too well their failures and shortcomings, but they have the confidence that no matter how miserably they behave, they can never, ever exile themselves beyond the reach of God's love and forgiveness."

Jesus brought God right into the center of our lives and taught us to call him not just 'Father' but 'Abba', which in Jesus' time was the most affectionate and familiar way that a child could address his or her father.

'Abba' in Aramaic means 'papa' or 'daddy'. Successful Catholics are conscious of that intuitive knowledge that God is our 'papa', our 'daddy'. And if God is indeed a loving father, he couldn't possibly be any less loving than the best earthly father. He couldn't possibly turn his back on or disown his child — no matter what.

Successful Catholics know this in the deepest part of their being. They are sure of forgiveness, of being able to start fresh. Like the author, Paul Wilkes, says: "God has a very short memory of our failings."

It's not this knowledge alone that makes a Catholic or any human being successful — it's how this knowledge transforms us. Once we can feel in the depths of our being how very much we are loved by God, it is the most natural thing for us to love him, to love others, and to love ourselves in that same way. And by loving like this, we are living the Gospel.

I believe that all the evil committed by people would never happen if those people were able to feel how much they were loved by God. It would be impossible to commit evil and to hurt others if we felt the depth of God's love for us.

It is my own personal belief that God finds a way to save everyone. That no human soul, no matter how evil the deed, is ever lost. That, in the end, God finds a way to get through. Maybe if we die unrepentant, God meets and sits down with us in a little room and shows us the whole panorama of our lives and all the hurtful and unloving and maybe even evil things we've done. And sitting there in the presence of this unconditionally loving father and witnessing the damage we've done to other people during our lives, our hearts are opened and we experience true remorse in the depths of our soul. And we turn to our Father and — of our own free will — we ask for forgiveness and are saved.

This concept might offend our sense of justice, but God's justice is not our justice. When we get to heaven and sit down with God for dinner, we may be surprised to see who else is at the table.

Jesus, through his presence in our world and through his Gospel, has made the knowledge of God's unconditional love available to everyone. The message that he left us in this Gospel book is simple; it can be summed up in three words: *We are loved.*

November 1997
Ordinary Time

Corpus Christi

Mark 14: 22 -24

While they were eating, he took some bread, and after a blessing he broke it, and gave it to them, and said, "Take it; this is my body." And when he had taken a cup and given thanks, he gave it to them, and they all drank from it. And he said to them, "This is my blood of the covenant . . ."

*

Today is the feast of Corpus Christi, the Body of Christ. Where is the Body of Christ?

The disciples on Easter morning frantically looked for the body of Christ. They were dazed and confused. But Jesus didn't want them — or us — going off on some treasure hunt, some wild goose chase. I don't think he would have been happy if CBS or NBC came up with some new reality show with Regis Philbin called *Who Wants to Find the Savior*. No, Jesus told us flat out where we could find his body, his *physical* presence. But he also gave us a wonderful gift, the gift of his *sacramental* presence in the Eucharist.

Jesus, by his own words, his own intentions, remains very present in the world. Both *physically* present where we can converse with him, walk with him, hold him, embrace him; and *sacramentally* present in the Eucharist where he can continue to nourish our souls.

Let's consider that *sacramental* presence first. Jesus left us a wonderful gift, in the Eucharist. Those men and women who celebrated that Passover meal, that Last Supper with Jesus, didn't at the time have a clue what Jesus was doing for them and for us. Here we are 2,000 years later in New Jersey still sharing that meal with Jesus. Each time that I am privileged to stand at the altar while the celebrant consecrates the bread and the wine, I feel like I am being transported by a time machine. The sanctuary becomes surreal, almost dreamlike, and I find myself back in that Upper Room in Jerusalem as Jesus is breaking the bread and sharing the cup.

We are very fortunate as Catholics to have our faith centered on the Eucharist. I remember my first communion very vividly, and that wonderful feeling of embracing Jesus remains with us throughout our life journey.

As a deacon, I have been privileged to share in many deeply personal moments in the lives of others — moments of sadness and moments of joy. But no moment is as special as the moment when I look into your eyes, my sisters and brothers, hand you the Eucharist and say, "the Body of Christ." At that moment, time and space stand still. What a joy to be present as you embrace Our Lord. What a privilege to be present at this moment of communion.

The Eucharist is a wonderful gift. But Jesus is still here among us *physically* in plain sight. We pass him every single day. If you're like me you probably walk right by most of the time without recognizing him.

[Then the righteous will answer him, "Lord, when did we see you hungry, and feed you, or thirsty, and give you something to drink? And when did we see you a stranger, and invite you in, or naked, and clothe you? When did we see you sick, or in prison, and come to you?" The King will answer and say to them, "Truly I say to you, to the extent that you did it to one of these brothers of mine, even the least of them, you did it to me."]

Matthew 25: 37 – 40

If Jesus walked the earth today in the year 2000 I can imagine him adding these words:

I was difficult to get along with and you remained my friend and continued to love me;

I was an unborn child and you not only protested for my right to life but sheltered and guided my unwed mother; and adopted me and loved me as your own;

I was unfaithful and betrayed your trust and you forgave me and gave me another chance;

I was the victim of violence, hatred, bigotry, ridicule or discrimination because I was gay, or because I was Jewish, or black or Asian or female and you stood by my side and were a voice for justice;

I was locked generation after generation in a cycle of poverty and dependence and you not only gave me your tax dollars but you gave me your time, your energy, your wisdom and guidance, and taught me to be productive and to break the cycle of dependence on the state;

I was on death row and you spared my life and showed me the unconditional forgiveness of the Father.

Corpus Christi, my brothers and sisters, the body of Christ.

So as we enjoy this beautiful day, this feast of the Body of Christ, let us thank God for the wonderful gift of Christ's body present to us *sacramentally* in the Eucharist. And let us equally cherish, embrace and soothe the body of Christ present to us *physically* in our neighbor — in the poor, in the socially outcast and in all those people, lovable and difficult, with whom we journey through life.

June 2000
Feast of Corpus Christi

New Year's Eve

Ever since I was a little boy I've been in love with the month of September. September has always symbolized a new beginning, a fresh start, a second chance to heal whatever is broken in our lives. This excitement and sense of renewal probably goes back to the start of each new school year and all the enthusiasm that went with it. But for all the many, many years that I've been out of school, I've never lost my love for September and the chance to start fresh one more time.

As part of this annual rebirth each September, I always go through a sort of long New Year's Eve so to speak. It usually starts around now, mid August. It is a time for reflection; a time to look deep within and ask myself if there are still any obstacles to God's unconditional love that I am refusing to let go of. As human beings, one of the biggest of these obstacles can be anger — anger that we might harbor for being hurt or abandoned by someone we loved and trusted very deeply.

Jesus says that when someone hurts us we must forgive. He tells us that the greatest gift we can give to another person and to ourselves is the gift of forgiveness. Forgiveness is the act of letting go of the past and accepting someone back into our heart; of extending our hand and allowing ourselves once more to be vulnerable to another. Jesus tells us that we must forgive unconditionally — that there can be no bounds, no strings, no limits to the amount of times we let someone back into our heart.

To genuinely forgive someone in the way that Jesus calls for, we must be willing to accept the reality that a person's faults and personality quirks will probably not disappear overnight. Jesus asks us to forgive even when the person who hurt us is not sorry; or even when we know that despite someone's sincere apology they are likely to hurt us again. He asks us to look into the eyes of someone who has hurt us deeply and to show that someone love and acceptance instead of anger and rejection.

To forgive is a choice that God gives us. When we forgive, we choose life, and love and a relationship for ourselves and for others. We relieve ourselves of the burden of carrying around hurt, pain and anger. By so doing we are opening the door for true healing to occur; healing within ourselves; healing within another; and maybe even healing of a relationship. And we give someone else the freedom to live their life — or maybe to rest in peace — with the knowledge that they are loved without strings.

So as we walk through these remaining days of August, this long New Year's Eve, let us ask God for the gift of forgiveness for any hurts we may have inflicted on others; and let us pray for the grace to forgive and to reach out to others to heal whatever remains broken in our lives.

August 1997
Ordinary Time

September 11th

I'm sure I have plenty of company when I tell you that since September 11th I haven't slept very well; there's been numbness and a sense of depression. When those planes flew into the World Trade Center they also made a gaping hole right through our hearts. The safe and secure world that we thought we knew, and maybe took for granted, was taken away. In its place is sadness, anxiety and a deep sense of mourning for so many lives lost: lost at Ground Zero, lost in Pennsylvania, in Washington, in Queens (whatever the cause) and in Afghanistan.

I believe that the enemy we face is pure evil. If flying planes filled with innocent people into buildings filled with innocent people, and claiming to do it in the name of God isn't evil, than nothing is evil. I also believe that we must defend ourselves and rid the world of this evil. And, at the same time, consistent with statements made by our President and by our Holy Father, we need to examine the environment that enabled this evil to grow and, in the process, to reevaluate our position in the Middle East, and our commitment to justice and statehood for those people who have had their homes and neighborhoods ripped away from them over the last 50 years.

Along with the Catholic bishops of the U.S., I believe we are engaged in a necessary and just war. Not a war of revenge, not a war of ideology or economics, but a war to make the world safe for my children, your children and the future of our human family; a war in which our government is doing its best to avoid inevitable civilian casualties and to respect human rights.

But I also listened to the gospel over the last few weeks and heard Jesus say things like: "Blessed are the peacemakers", "Love your enemy", "Turn the other cheek", "Do not resist those who try to hurt you." And, if I am to be honest with myself, I think that if Jesus were here he would not approve of what we are doing.

So, the position of the U.S. bishops notwithstanding, I — perhaps like many of you — have been facing a serious moral conflict.

God calls us to do our best, to balance the inevitable conflicts and challenges we face in our lives and to persevere. There is no easy answer to moral conflict; just like there is no easy answer to the cross. Both are contradictions.

And yet in the center of the cross, in the center of the contradiction, we will always find God — if we look hard enough. God is with us through all our contradictions, through all our failings and successes. He just asks that we not give up.

Two people who persevered and didn't give up are Heather Mercer and Dayna Curry. Along with six other international relief workers, they were imprisoned in August by the Taliban and charged with preaching Christianity, with telling people in Afghanistan about Jesus. They faced possible death sentences for the crime of being Christians.

I watched a CNN special on both women two weeks ago. They have incredible faith and deep joy for life. They put their belief in the Gospel into action and went into the most dangerous situation to help others. In an interview after their rescue on Wednesday, both women joyfully said they want to return to work with the poor of Afghanistan.

When I heard the news that these women had been rescued that part of my spirit which has felt so crushed since Sept. 11th came back to life.

Jesus calls us to persevere. In many ways he asks us to have the faith and the courage of 30 year old Dayna and 24 year old Heather.

Let us pray that in the midst of fear and devastation we are able to persevere in our faith and our love for others. And in the months and years ahead, let us continually ask ourselves this question: if it ever were to become a crime to be a Christian, could there be enough evidence brought forward to convict us?

September 2002
Ordinary Time

Our Mission

Today we are celebrating the birthday of Saint John the Baptist. John was sent into the world by God with a special mission. He planted him in Judea at the time of Jesus. His mission was to lead people to Christ and help them experience the presence of God in their lives.

And like John, our loving Creator has sent each of us into world with a mission. He planted us in the many circles of our lives — there are no accidents. We are spouses, parents, siblings, children, workers, bosses, priests, sisters, teachers, friends, even strangers sitting next to each other on a bus. These are the circles of our lives; these are the places where we are called to live out our mission.

Our mission is like John's. We have been sent to help people experience the presence of God in their lives. Those people are our family and friends, our co-workers, even the stranger on the bus. But we can't be faithful to our mission if we are angry or negative people. We can't be faithful to our mission if we put down, exclude or reject others because they don't live up to our standards. We can only be faithful to our mission if we love others the way God does — unconditionally, for who they are and where they are.

That doesn't mean that we condone their actions if they hurt others. It doesn't mean that we allow ourselves to be doormats or victims. Loving unconditionally means that we never shut down our hearts; that we are always there to love, forgive and help others experience God's love through us.

As we remember John the Baptist, let us open the doors and windows of our hearts and enable God's love to flow through us to each and every person we meet in the circles of our lives.

June 2007
Nativity of John the Baptist

Away in the Manger

Over the last few years there's been a lot of controversy about the Christmas manger. Some towns and municipalities permit nativity displays on public property. Some forbid it, believing it infringes on the rights of others and crosses the line between church and state. I don't know about you, but I find it easy to get offended by this.

It's easy to get angry that we can't put Baby Jesus on display for everyone to see. But the reality is that we are always 100% free to display the Christ child anywhere and anytime. I can't speak for any of you, but I, only too often, keep him hidden away — wrapped tightly in the swaddling clothes of my own ego and prejudice.

You see, we are all like that little manger in Bethlehem, because within each of us there is the presence of Christ. Christ lives within us and we are called to unwrap him for the world to see. We don't need a public display in the town square to make Christ present in the world.

The true public display of Christian faith is how we live our lives — how we love God and treat others. Are we kind and forgiving, or do we carry a grudge? Are we inclusive, non-judgmental and accepting, or do we shut people out of our lives because they are different or don't measure up to our moral standards? Are our doors and our phones always open, or are there family members and friends whom we have shut out of our hearts and out of our lives because of some real or imaginary slight that we can't even remember?

Christmas is not just about shopping at Neiman Marcus and Target and going to holiday parties. Christmas is not just about nativity displays. Christmas is about unwrapping the Christ child within and enabling others to experience the presence of Christ through us.

As we journey through Advent, let us recognize, unwrap and embrace the Christ child within us. Let us reach out with unconditional love to those who are estranged and absent from our lives. Let us make Christ truly present in all the circles of our lives. That presence is far more real than any ceramic statue in the town square.

December 2007
Advent

Ashes to Ashes

Ashes to ashes, dust to dust. "Remember you are dust and to dust you will return."

These are the words that we hear on Ash Wednesday as the door opens for us onto one more season of Lent. They are meant to remind us that all things are changing, only God's love is forever; and that the purpose of our life is to manifest God's love here in our world: to share it with others and return it to its sender.

When each of us was conceived, God breathed his love into the beginnings of what would become our earthly body. That breath of God is our soul. It is a part of God, just like a wave is part of the ocean. It is meant to find its way home to its creator; it is meant to live with God forever.

Our minds, our hopes and anxieties, our careers, our treasures — along with our earthy bodies — will all pass away. Ashes to ashes, dust to dust. In the end, the only thing that will have mattered is how well we have loved.

The soul comes into the world with the instinct to love. It is the natural law of God imprinted on our DNA. All people, whatever their beliefs or lack of beliefs, carry this imprint and are called to return home to God. As followers of Jesus we have the benefit of a blueprint, an owner's manual, a GPS that shows us how to live, how to love, how to get home.

That blueprint is the Gospel. Jesus lays it out in detail in the Sermon on the Mount, the Beatitudes. And when the Pharisees asked him what was the greatest commandment of all, he summed it up for them and for us: "Love God with your whole heart and your whole mind and your whole soul, and love others — love others — as you love yourself."

This Lent, as we sacrifice some little pleasures, some things we really enjoy, let us remember what really matters. Let us sit before God in the Blessed Sacrament and ponder how well we are following Jesus' blueprint in the Gospel. In the end, the only thing that will have mattered is how well we have loved while we were alive.

God is love. And to quote the songwriter Carole King: "Only love is real, everything else an illusion."

February 2008
Lent

The Universe is God's Family Business

Matthew 7: 21

(Jesus said to his disciples): "Not everyone who says to me, 'Lord, Lord' will enter the kingdom of heaven, but he who does the will of my Father."

*

I went on retreat for a day and heard a Jesuit priest tell us that the universe is God's family business. So I think of it now as 'GodandSon.com'. God made it with the hope that it would one day grow into a garden filled with peace and love; a place that would be known from one end to the other as the Kingdom of God. But God won't get what he wants unless we accept his invitation to come into the family business, and work with his son to build that Kingdom.

Building the Kingdom of God takes more than just prayer, more than just saying, 'Lord, Lord'. It takes more than just coming to church or reading the Bible. It takes listening to Jesus' words in the Gospel and acting on them, making them come alive in all the circles of our lives. But his message was hard to hear back then, and it's hard to hear today: Love unconditionally; forgive unconditionally; turn the other cheek when someone strikes us; treat every human being like we would treat Christ himself.

Building the Kingdom of God takes more than just saying, 'Lord, Lord'. We are called to be pure of heart and deed, but we are also called to reject the structures of sin in our society; to recognize the sin inherent in neglect of the poor and the sick; in discrimination, racism, sexism, anti-Semitism, homophobia, bigotry in all its forms — and to stand up against these social sins.

We are called to respect the sanctity of life but we are also called to promote a seamless culture of life; to be vocal advocates not just for the unborn, but for the residents of death row and the undocumented refugee as well. We are called to treat the least, most vulnerable, most unlovable member of society just like we would treat Jesus himself. Jesus wasn't kidding around in the Gospel; and he wasn't just making suggestions. Building the Kingdom of God takes more than just saying, 'Lord, Lord'. Are we kind and peaceful, or do we carry around anger and bitterness? Are we gentle and forgiving of ourselves, or do we bring the burden of self-loathing, whether it is conscious or unconscious, into every relationship we have? Are our doors always open, or are there people whom we have shut out of our hearts and out of our lives because of some deep hurt or disappointment that we just can't forgive? Are we inclusive, non-judgmental and accepting, or do we look down upon or feel morally superior to others because they are different from us, or represent something we fear or dislike? We can't be about God's family business unless we are building his Kingdom.

'Lord, Lord,' is a nice salutation but Jesus never stood on formality. Instead, he is counting on us to help him turn the universe into a beautiful garden for his dad, a garden filled with peace and love, a place that will be known from one end to the other as the Kingdom of God. Let us be mindful as we open our eyes on each new day that God is once again calling us to join him and his son in the family business.

June 2008
Ordinary Time

Love is the Greatest Talent

Matthew 25: 1, 14 – 18

(Then the kingdom of Heaven will be) . . . "like a man about to go on a journey, who called his own slaves and entrusted his possessions to them. To one he gave five talents, to another, two, and to another, one, each according to his own ability; and he went on his journey. Immediately the one who had received the five talents went and traded with them, and gained five more talents. In the same manner the one who had received the two talents gained two more. But he who received the one talent went away, and dug a hole in the ground and hid his master's money."

*

Some people can sing, others can design and build amazing things; some are gifted artists, others eloquent speakers. But there is one basic talent that each one of us comes into the world with — the ability to love others unconditionally.

Ultimately, when all is said and done, the value of our life here on earth and the measure by which we will be judged, is not how well we sang, or built, or painted, or spoke, but how well and how much we have loved others.

This represents your life:

The heart in the center is you. The concentric circles are the circles of your life — the many gardens in which God has planted you; the circles in which we journey with other souls who are special to us. Those circles are different for each of us.

For me the inner circle is for my wife, my soul mate Wanda. The next circle is for my four best friends, my four children — Danny, David, Julie and Meg.

The next is for my very close friends. The next is for members of our parish community, my colleagues and associates at work, and so on.

Think for a moment — who lives in the circles of your life?

In each of those circles there are windows. When you open those windows, you allow God's love to flow through you to each person who lives there. When you open those windows, you open your heart. And when you open your heart, you are using that one basic talent that God made you for. But when your heart is closed, you have buried that talent in the ground.

I believe that when we die we sit with God in a little room and look through those windows. It will be an accounting of how well and how much we have loved the people in the circles of our lives.

I pray for myself and for each of you that when we sit there with God there are no closed windows; there are no people whom we have shut out, or closed our hearts to. If there are, today is a very good day to go home and open them up again.

November 2002
Ordinary Time

God Lives in the Ordinary

John 2: 1 – 3, 5 - 11

On the third day there was a wedding in Cana of Galilee, and the mother of Jesus was there; and both Jesus and his disciples were invited to the wedding. When the wine ran out, the mother of Jesus said to him, "They have no wine." . . . His mother said to the servants, "Whatever he says to you, do it." Now there were six stone waterpots set there for the Jewish custom of purification . . . Jesus said to them, "Fill the waterpots with water." So they filled them up to the brim. And he said to them, "Draw some out now and take it to the headwaiter." So they took it to him. When the headwaiter tasted the water which had become wine . . . (he) called the bridegroom, and said to him, "Every man serves the good wine first, and when the people have drunk freely, then he serves the poorer wine; but you have kept the good wine until now." This beginning of his signs Jesus did in Cana of Galilee, and manifested his glory, and his disciples believed in him.

*

God lives in the ordinary. We don't have to jump through hoops to find him. It's not necessary to wash our hands a hundred times or to take off our shoes before we approach him. He is present in the everyday things we do — in the smell of a flower, the warmth of the sun, in a kiss between lovers, in the smile of a child. God is present in the ordinary time of our life.

How many of you know why Father and I are wearing green vestments today? Well, green symbolizes that the Church has entered the cycle of the year that we call Ordinary Time. And green was chosen because it represents life, ordinary life, in its full bloom: trees, fields, leaves, grass. Today's Gospel story is very fitting as we begin this cycle of the Church year.

The Gospel writer sets the stage in ordinary time. Jesus didn't choreograph his first miracle to happen in the town square at some major political event or religious feast. It wasn't done at Passover or the Festival of Lights where CNN could cover it and give him maximum exposure. Actually, he didn't even plan to start doing miracles that day. He had to be coaxed by his mom — a fact that in itself is endearing. Jesus worked his first miracle spontaneously and in a very ordinary setting, a wedding. Not only does this story show us that Jesus thought highly of marriage, it shows us that he was present to people in a very ordinary way.

There is a symbolic message in the story too — the waterpots. Jewish ritual and law required guests to purify their hands and feet before eating so as not to defile themselves. In the story these waterpots represent all the burdens, rituals and guilt that people feel they have to deal with to be acceptable to God. Jesus' turning that ritualistic water into wine for celebrating with the young couple tells us that we approach God, not through repetitive ritual or guilt, but in the ordinary acts of love and celebrating life.

The Gospel tells us to look for God right where we are — not to run around with obsession or compulsion; not to be focused on guilt or anxiety, but to find God in the people we love, the friends we work with, in the ordinary water that flows though the fabric of our life.

February 2002
Ordinary Time

Essence

The essence of our Catholic faith is Jesus; his Presence to us in the Eucharist; and his call to us to love God, to love each other and to be beacons of light and conduits of God's for our world. Everything else is system, process, and structure — designed and managed by human beings. As a computer systems professional I know that every system has points of failure; every process has flaws; and every structure chips away and eventually falls apart to be replaced by something better, stronger but destined to again be replaced in the endless cycle of quality improvement. But the essence never changes.

In those periods of transition from old system to new system, there is upset and turmoil. It's tough enough when it's a payroll system, or an accounting system, or a hospital billing system. But when the system is our institutional Church, and when the process is trust, the period of transition is emotionally very painful. It is in these emotionally painful times that the Holy Spirit is most closely guiding us.

The system, the process and the structure of our Roman Catholic Church is going through a painful time. It is a period of sadness, disappointment and anger; but the essence of our Catholic faith has not changed one iota. The essence continues to be Jesus and his call to action for us to love God, to love each other and to be beacons of light for our world.

When we are hurt and disappointed, it is very tempting to think of the Church as something out there. But the Church does not live exclusively behind closed doors in Rome or in Boston or in L.A. It is just as alive in these pews, and in the base communities of Latin America, and in the underground Masses secretly held in Communist China.

Each member of the Church, from the Pope to this little baby here, is a beautiful piece in an overall mosaic — and that mosaic is the Body of Christ. Looked at as a whole, we are the Body of Christ, we are the Church.

And as Church, as pieces of the mosaic and members of the Body of Christ, we cannot lose heart; we must follow through on Jesus' call to action even in the most difficult periods of institutional sadness and transition.

During these current difficult times it is our responsibility — to the best of our ability — to reach out with healing, compassion and justice to those young people who have been victims of evil and betrayal at the hands of a few; to require accountability and conscientious management from our leaders; to encourage, support, and stand by the overwhelming majority of our priests who are living dedicated, holy and loving lives.

Even though we are going through a difficult time, we cannot let our light be dampened. Jesus' call to us to bring God's love into the world doesn't just apply to sunny days when our institutional house is in order. Our world is facing great danger — perhaps the greatest ever faced; from the imminent threat of further acts of terrorism; to the stand-off on the border of India and Pakistan; to the anguish of death that pervades the marketplaces of Israel and the refugee camps of the Palestinians. That light of Jesus within us, the essence of our Catholic faith, needs to burn brighter now than ever before. We are the Church; we are the Body of Christ.

October 2002
Ordinary Time

Into the Deep

Luke 5: 2, 4 – 6, 8, 10 - 11

(Jesus) saw two boats lying at the edge of the lake; but the fishermen had gotten out of them and were washing their nets . . . He said to Simon, "Put out into the deep water and let down your nets for a catch." Simon answered and said, "Master, we worked hard all night and caught nothing, but I will do as you say and let down the nets." When they had done this, they enclosed a great quantity of fish, and their nets began to break . . . But when Simon Peter saw that, he fell down at Jesus' feet, saying, "Go away from me Lord, for I am a sinful man! . . ." And Jesus said to Simon, "Do not fear, from now on you will be catching men." When they had brought their boats to land, they left everything and followed him.

*

It must have been a pretty sorry day in Galilee. Peter and his buddies had worked hard all night and didn't have as much as a guppy or a goldfish to show for it. Tired, depressed and feeling like failures, they climb out of their boat and dragged themselves and their nets ashore.

As they finish washing their nets, they see Jesus smiling at them. He tells them to put their disappointment, their discouragement aside; to let go of their emptiness and negativity, and to trust in him. He tells them to put out into the deep and lower their nets. And once they take this leap of faith, the emptiness and the negativity disappear, and their nets become filled to capacity.

Some of us may have dragged ourselves through these doors this morning, like Peter and his friends, carrying emptiness and negativity in our hearts. Maybe the loss of a loved one, or a relationship, or a job; maybe some bad news back from a biopsy; maybe some anger, hurt or resentment we've been carrying around for many years.

But we came here to Mass, and Jesus speaks to us through today's Gospel. He tells us that it's time for us to put out into the deep and lower our nets; to let go of any anger, anxiety, depression, self-loathing that haunts us; to make room in our hearts for God's love.

Jesus calls us to lower our nets. But like, Peter, we need to say 'yes'. We need to trust Jesus enough to put out into the deep. It is only our 'yes', our willingness to let go, that will enable us to be filled to capacity with God's love and to share that love with others.

February 2007
Ordinary Time

Prepare Ye the Way of the Lord

Luke 3: 2 – 4

. . . the word of God came to John, the son of Zacharias, in the wilderness. And he came into all the district around the Jordan, preaching a baptism of repentance for the forgiveness of sins . . . "(Prepare Ye) . . . the way of the Lord."

*

My all time favorite musical is *Godspell*. Have any of you seen it? My wife and I went to see the original off-Broadway production way back in 1971. We saw the movie version in 1974 and bought the video when it was released. In 1987, 1995, 2000, and most recently this October, *Godspell* was performed on stages in New York and New Jersey. Not only did Wanda and I go to these performances, but we brought family members, co-workers and special friends to share in this wonderful experience.

Godspell is a musical rendition of the Gospel of Saint Matthew set in modern day New York City. Jesus is portrayed as a loving, warm and energetic figure with a great sense of humor. He wears a Superman shirt, sneakers and has a heart drawn in greasepaint on his forehead. He gathers a ragtag group of disciples from the streets, the subways, the parks and office buildings; together they sing and dance their way through the parables and ultimately through the crucifixion to the resurrection.

The movie version opens with John the Baptist walking across an empty Brooklyn Bridge at dawn, calling the world to conversion. He is pushing a tinker's cart and singing "Prepare Ye the Way of the Lord!" The movie ends with the disciples carrying the crucified body of Jesus down a deserted early morning street. They are singing the same song, "Prepare Ye the Way of the Lord!"

They reach a deserted corner that looks like it could be Park Avenue and E. 60th Street. They turn the corner and are out of sight, but you can still hear them singing. As the camera turns the corner you can no longer see the disciples carrying Jesus. All you can see are the faces of hundreds of oncoming, everyday, ordinary people just like you and me rushing about their business.

Each time I see this movie and the camera turns that corner, I am filled with emotion. I can see the risen Christ present in each of those oncoming faces. And I am thankful that I, like each of you, have been called as a disciple to prepare the way of the Lord in our world.

Today's Gospel brings to mind John the Baptist pushing his tinker's cart across the Brooklyn Bridge and calling us to conversion. But conversion is not a one time event. We are called to conversion and to renewal everyday of our lives. Conversion is not a matter of believing the right thing; it's a matter of loving, forgiving, listening and being present: Present to God, present to our children, our spouse, our friends, and to all those we meet along the way. Conversion is a lifelong journey — one on which we frequently trip and fall down.

But God gives us time to get it right. Each new day is a new beginning, a gift from God, a 'do over' — a chance to forgive, to love, to be kind.

As we experience Advent this year, let us hear the voice of John the Baptist calling us to conversion; calling us to love, to forgive, to be kind; to reach out and reconcile with those whom we may not have spoken to in years because we are harboring some anger or resentment; calling us to Prepare the Way of the Lord in our own lives. And let us recommit ourselves as disciples to follow Jesus with singing and dancing and joy through the rush hour of life.

December 2006
Advent

The Prodigal Son

Luke 15:11-32

(Jesus) said, "A man had two sons. The younger of them said to his father, 'Father, give me the share of the estate that falls to me.' So he divided his wealth between them. And not many days later, the younger son gathered everything together and went on a journey into a distant country, and there he squandered his estate with loose living. Now when he had spent everything, a severe famine occurred in that country and he began to be impoverished. So he went and hired himself out to one of citizens of that country, and he sent him into his fields to feed swine. And he would have gladly filled his stomach with the pods that the swine were eating, and no one was giving anything to him. But when he came to his senses, he said, 'How many of my father's hired men have more than enough bread, but I am dying here with hunger! I will get up and go to my father, and will say to him, "Father, I have sinned against heaven, and in your sight; I am no longer worthy to be called your son; make me as one of your hired men."' So he got up and came to his father. But while he was still a long way off, his father saw him and felt compassion for him, and ran and embraced him and kissed him. And the son says to him, 'Father, I have sinned against

heaven and in your sight; I am no longer worthy to be called your son.'
But the father said to his slaves, 'Quickly bring out the best robe and put
it on him, and put a ring on his hand and sandals on his feet; and bring
the fattened calf, kill it, and let us eat and celebrate; for this son of mine
was dead and has come to life again; he was lost and has been found.'
And they began to celebrate. Now his older son was in the field, and
when he came and approached the house, he heard music and dancing.
And he summoned one of the servants and began inquiring what these
things could be. And he said to him, 'Your brother has come, and your
father has killed the fattened calf because he has received him back safe
and sound.' But he became angry and was not willing to go in; and his
father came out and began pleading with him. But he answered and said
to his father, 'Look! For so many years I have been serving you and I
have never neglected a command of yours; and yet you have never given
me a young goat, so that I might celebrate with my friends; but when
this son of yours came, who has devoured your wealth with prostitutes,
you killed the fattened calf for him.' And he said to him, 'Son, you have
always been with me, and all that is mine is yours. But we had to
celebrate and rejoice, for this brother of yours was dead and has begun
to live, and was lost and has been found.'"

*

God loves us deeply. When we turn away from him he forgives
and pursues us until we come home. This is how deeply God expects us
to love each other.

When God made me and you he embraced each one of us like a
mother would bundle up a beloved child to go out into the cold for the
very first time. And like a parent might slip a little identification note
into a child's pocket, just in case he or she should get lost, God put a
little piece of himself inside of us. That little piece of God inside of you
and me is our immortal soul. And life is the journey of our soul back
home to God.

God loves us so much that he takes a great risk: he sets us free
for our journey. He gives us free will — the freedom to say 'yes' or 'no'
to his love. And with that freedom comes the possibility that we might
not come home. So during our journey, God cannot sleep. Just like those
of you parents with teenage drivers in the family, God waits anxiously
by the window, watching for us to get home safely.

We can only make it home safely by saying 'yes' to God — by living the gospel as Jesus taught us and genuinely loving God and other people. It's hard to say 'yes' to God if we carry around anger and bitterness; if we are unforgiving and have shut people out of our lives. It's hard to say 'yes' to God if we look down on or feel morally superior to someone or some group because they are different from us, or represent something we dislike or fear. It's hard to say 'yes' to God when our faith has been shaken by events around us. Yet even when we say 'no', God forgives and pursues to bring us back home.

In today's Gospel the first son said 'no' when he took his share of his inheritance. He left home and squandered everything. The second son said 'no' when he stewed in his resentment and refused to enter the house to welcome his brother home. But the father loves his sons equally. He forgives and pursues them both. He would not rest until the first son who was lost came home, and he would not celebrate and experience joy until the second son let go of his resentment, his anger and came home as well.

Jesus' point with this parable is twofold: to tell us how eager God is to forgive us and welcome us back into his heart; and to show us how *we* are to say 'yes' to life, to love and to God.

It's not easy to say 'yes' on this anniversary of September 11th. Three years ago everything changed forever. It's not easy to say 'yes' when we pick up a newspaper or turn on the news and see suffering, violence, and hatred. But our loving Father is anxiously waiting by that window and watching for us to come home safely. And if we continue to follow Jesus and keep saying 'yes', someday each one of us will hear those most wonderful words, "Welcome home, my beloved child."

September 2004
Ordinary Time

Time

Luke 21: 5 – 6

And while some were talking about the temple, that it was adorned with beautiful stones and votive gifts . . . (Jesus) said, "As for these things which you are looking at, the day will come in which there will not be left one stone upon another which will not be torn down."

Will you and I be ready to face that day when it comes?

*

Next weekend we will celebrate the feast of Christ the King. It is the last Sunday in the Liturgical calendar and marks the end of the Church year. The Church has been preparing us for this over the last few weeks with readings and Gospels that speak about the last days, the end of time as we know it.

We can look at today's Gospel as a prophecy about the end of the world. We can see it as foretelling a cataclysmic moment in human history when the righteous will be swept up to heaven in rapture and the not-so-righteous will be swallowed up into hell. Or, we can see it as a wake up call, a reminder that, through our Baptism, each one of us has been hired by Jesus to be a construction worker, a builder, of the Kingdom of God — and time is running out.

No one knows how and when the world will end. What we do know is that time, our own unique, individual time, will end some day. The end of the world will come for each of us at the moment we cross the threshold of life into death. And when our end time does come, we will have to account for what we did — and what we failed to do — with the precious time we were given.

I believe that when we die each one of us will sit alone in a little room with God and watch the movie of our life. And in that movie we will see where we loved and where we failed to love. And sitting there next to God, the source of all goodness and love, we will judge ourselves — on how much we loved, really loved; how much we forgave, really forgave; how inclusive and accepting we were; how much we helped others to find goodness and wholeness in their own lives, their own unique circumstances.

The Church, in preparing us for the end of the year with these readings, is helping us call to mind our own mortality, our own inevitable end time. None of us knows how much time we have left. Each morning, as we open our eyes, God gives us 1,440 brand new minutes to use. We can use them with love to heal our world and our relationships with others; or we can waste them in self-centeredness, bitterness and anger.

The great thing about the end of the Church year and the reminder about the end times, is that we still do have time — time to love, time to forgive, time to come outside of ourselves and be present to others. We have this gift of time to fix whatever is still broken in our lives; to heal any damaged relationships; to make ourselves whole.

Like Jesus says in today's Gospel, "All that you see here — the day will come when there will not be left a stone upon another stone." We don't know when the end of the world will come, but we do know that it will come for each of us. And when that day does come, all that will remain for eternity is the love that we shared while we still had time.

November 2004
Ordinary Time

The Problem of Evil

Matthew 5: 2 - 4

When Jesus saw the crowds, he went up on the mountain . . . and began to teach them, saying . . . "Blessed are those who mourn, for they shall be comforted."

*

Like many of you I struggle with the problem of evil: if God is all powerful and all loving, and really does know and love each one of us, why does he allow such terrible things to happen?

My heart broke as I watched CNN over the last six months and heard the cries of hostages in Iraq: the young Korean man, close in age and appearance to my own son, who pleaded for his life for days before being so savagely murdered; the men from America and the UK working as contractors in a war torn country, begging to see their families again; and Margaret Hassan, good and loving Margaret Hassan, a modern saint who dedicated her life for 30 years as the head of operations for *Care* in Iraq, looking into the camera and weeping the day before she was brutally executed. And yet Jesus tells us, "Blessed are they who mourn," — we who mourn — for we will be comforted — someday, someplace, somehow, it will all make sense.

My soul ached: as I watched the news and saw the despair of a father from Sweden who heard his three year old son cry, "Daddy, I'm scared," as the tsunami ripped him from his father's arms forever; as I saw the agony of a 14 year old Palestinian boy whose spine was severed and his eye destroyed by a mortar fired into a refugee camp; as I read the names and the ages of our boys and girls — our men and women — who will never come home from war. And yet Jesus tells us, "Blessed are they who mourn," for someday, someplace, somehow, it will all make sense.

These acts of human evil and natural disaster don't mean that God doesn't love us or that he isn't present to us. Life is a mystery, like a tapestry that we cannot see fully while we are in the middle of it. But God is with us in the mystery and brings good out of evil. Even if we cannot see it in this life, there is something more than meets the eye. There's a life to come where those of us who mourn will indeed be comforted.

But while we are here, the cross is our comfort and our answer to the problem of evil. It is a sign that God is with us in our suffering and that death is not the end. When we read the Passion and hear Jesus' cry, "My God, why have you forsaken me?" we know that he understands what we are going through; that he is our brother in the face of horrible evil. Our brother, our savior who takes us — the temporary prisoners of evil — through the sufferings of life; who leads us to the joy of resurrection; to a place where everything will make sense and we will see God.

Blessed are we who mourn, for we will be comforted.

.

February 2005
Ordinary Time

.

The Harvest is Abundant in Everyday Life

Matthew 9: 35 – 38

Jesus was going through all the cities and villages, teaching in their synagogues and proclaiming the Gospel of the kingdom, and healing every kind of disease and every kind of sickness. Seeing the people, he felt compassion for them, because they were distressed and dispirited like sheep without a shepherd. Then he said to his disciples,

"The harvest is plentiful, but the workers are few. Therefore beseech the Lord of the harvest to send out workers into his harvest."

*

The harvest is abundant in everyday life. From the Gospel we know that Jesus told his disciples to go out and cure the sick, cleanse lepers, drive out demons and raise the dead. But what the Gospel writer left out was the part about raising our kids, cherishing our spouse, doing our best at our job, and being present to our relatives and friends and the people we serve.

Cleansing lepers and driving out demons are valuable skills, especially in today's economy. Serving God as a nun, priest, brother or deacon are also wonderful and loving vocations. No less wonderful, no less loving, are the vocations of being a parent, a spouse, a sibling, a friend.

Our vocation in life is right where we are; where God has planted us. It takes faith, and love to drive out demons. But it takes faith, love, and stamina to raise a child to adulthood; to be a lifelong best friend and sweetheart to a spouse; to be a loving relative, friend, worker, or boss. It takes courage in today's society to be a priest, a nun, or a brother. These are our vocations. These are the places where God has planted us. The harvest of our vocation is abundant. That harvest is love.

Yes, raising the dead is a spectacular achievement. But raising our children, journeying through life with our spouse, working hard and honestly at our jobs and professions, serving tirelessly at the altar, seeing God's love in every relationship we have — those are vocations.

My sisters and brothers, the harvest is abundant in our everyday life.

June 2005
Ordinary Time

Faith is a Noun and a Verb

Matthew 17: 20

(Jesus said to them) ". . . if you have faith the size of a mustard seed, you will say to this mountain, 'Move from here to there,' and it will move; and nothing will be impossible to you."

*

I used to think that the word 'faith' was a noun, but I have come to understand that faith is both a noun and a verb. Faith is something that we proclaim as a community in prayer here at Mass, but faith does not come alive until we carry it out through the church door and live it day after day in the world.

> *Lex Orandi*
> *Lex Credendi*
> *Lex Vivendi*

I like this sign; not because it has my name in it, although that does appeal to me, but because it summarizes what it means to be a Catholic. "Lex Orandi, Lex Credendi, Lex Vivendi". Literally the Latin translates as *the law of prayer is the law of belief is the law of living.*
In modern English it means:

> *We Pray What We Believe*
> *We Live What We Pray*

This Latin adage was the guiding principle of the early Christian communities. It got lost somewhere around the Middle Ages, but was brilliantly restored by the Second Vatican Council in the 1960s. It is our call to action, our invitation to pray what we believe: that Christ has died, Christ has risen, and Christ will come again. And it is our charge to carry the belief that we pray here as a community out through the Church doors. It is our call to arms to live out our Eucharistic prayer by being the hands and feet and the voice of Christ in his mission to redeem the world.

The Second Vatican Council reminded Catholics that whatever we do in liturgy must "ritualize a lived reality." The bread and wine becoming the real presence of Christ on this altar only takes on meaning when that presence is made manifest in the world — especially to those most suffering and in need.

It is there in the world that our faith is transformed from a noun into a verb. It is there in the world that our faith is made active through *us*, with *us,* and in *us*, just as salvation is active through *Him*, with *Him*, and in *Him*.

One of the great Catholic theologians of our time Karl Rahner speaks of the three tables of the liturgy: the table of the word, the table of the Eucharist, and the table of the world. We come together here in community to be nourished with the Lord's word, and his body and blood, so that we might in turn go out into the streets, the offices, the factories, the schools, and the malls and bring that nourishment to the world.

Sister Mary Collins, another theologian, tells us about the "theology of the door." She calls us to come to terms with the church door — a door that swings both ways between the altar and the world. Our faith doesn't stop with the 'dismissal' at the end of Mass; it starts there. It comes alive when we go into the world and become Eucharist for others.

Faith can indeed move mountains, it can even uproot mulberry trees; but it first needs to be transformed from a noun to a verb. As we leave Church today, as we pass through that door, let us be mindful that we are moving from the table of the Eucharist to the table of the world — a world that needs redemption; a world that desperately needs each one of us to be the hands and the feet and the voice of Christ.

October 2005
Ordinary Time

Synchronicity as the Work of the Holy Spirit

The writers of the Old Testament had no knowledge of the Blessed Trinity and the person of the Holy Spirit. They were, however, very much aware of the Presence of God's Spirit in the world. And in writing the Old Testament they used the literary image of Wisdom as a personified feminine being to convey the experience of that divine Presence in their lives. In the Old Testament, Wisdom is what we Christians have come to know as the Holy Spirit.

The Second Vatican Council in the 1960s reawakened the consciousness of the Church to the active presence of the Holy Spirit in the world. The Council reminded all of us that it is through God's Spirit that we are led to truth and, ultimately, to salvation. Since the Council, the Church has urged us to be attentive and responsive to the promptings of the Holy Spirit in our lives; while at the same time cautioning us that those promptings can be difficult to discern.

Over the last year and a half I have been very much drawn to the Holy Spirit. As part of graduate studies in Pastoral Ministry, I have been researching ways in which, the Holy Spirit makes herself known to us. My thesis is that one way in which the Holy Spirit prompts us is through the experience of synchronicity.

The word 'synchronicity' is a term used by the psychologist Carl Jung to describe the experience of meaningful coincidences that are not causally related; coincidences that we experience as if God were winking at us, trying to get our attention, telling us that he is with us through all things. I have had these experiences, and whenever I speak about them people are quick to share their own. Our experiences of synchronicity are the promptings of the Holy Spirit at work in our lives.

As Catholics we believe in a God who loves each one of us as if we were the only person in the world; a God who is not content to stand in the wings, hoping and waiting for us to come home, but who passionately pursues us through life — like a 'hound of heaven' — lest we lose our way. Synchronistic events that occur throughout our life create a 'highway' on which the Holy Spirit travels to reach and guide us — but we must be attentive and responsive to these promptings.

Being attentive requires that we be truly present: present to God, present to others, and present to self. God can only be found in the present; not in what might have been, or what might be, but in what *is*. It is in the present, the now, that the Holy Spirit is always by our side, trying to get our attention, trying to show us the way.

November 2005
Ordinary Time

A Grain of Wheat

John 12: 23 – 24

And Jesus answered them, saying, "The hour has come for the Son of Man to be glorified. Truly, truly, I say to you, unless a grain of wheat falls into the earth and dies, it remains alone; but if it dies, it bears much fruit."

*

When we are conceived, God puts a little piece of himself inside us. That little piece of God is our immortal soul; it is the essence of who we are and the seed of what we will become — it is our true Self.

God places that soul into our human body. In order to navigate this body through life, we develop an ego. The ego gives us our sense of personal identity and relationship to others. It would be impossible to get through life without one. But where our soul is eternal, our ego is temporary. It can be an obstacle to our soul's development if we take it too seriously.

Jesus warns us against this in today's Gospel when he says, *"Unless a grain of wheat falls to the ground and dies, it remains just a grain of wheat; but if it dies, it bears much fruit."* The grain of wheat is our human ego. For our souls to produce real fruit for God, our egos have to figuratively fall to the ground.

During his life and through the Gospel, Jesus calls us to produce much fruit; to open our hearts with love and forgivingness to all those around us; to cherish and nurture the loved ones in our lives; to trust in God's love for us and to surrender ourselves to that love without fretting about the past or having anxiety about the future.

How often have we allowed our egos to close our hearts, and shut out a friend or relative who may have offended us, or not measured up to our moral standards? How often have we allowed our egos to waste our precious time and energies in the pursuit of false gods — like wealth, power, status and perfection — while our loved ones go wanting for our time and attention? How often have we allowed our egos to drag us into the quicksand of anxiety while the precious hours that God has given us slip away?

Lent is a very good time for us to let our egos fall to the ground. It is a time for us to unlock our hearts, to banish anger from our lives, and to reach out to those we have shut out. It is a time for us to reassess our priorities, and to redirect our time and our energies to our loved ones before it is too late. It is a time for us to take Jesus' hand and let him lift us up from anxiety.

Lent is an excellent time for our souls to produce much fruit for God.

April 2003
Lent

Signs in the Sun

Luke 21: 25

(Jesus said to his disciples), "There will be signs in sun and moon and stars, and on the earth dismay among nations . . ."

*

As Catholics, as Americans, as human beings, we live in difficult times. Every time I drive across the George Washington Bridge on a sunny day and look at the New York skyline, I remember a time that is gone forever.

Day after day I watch the news and read the papers and my heart is heavy. Heavy for the young soldiers who will never come home from Iraq and Afghanistan; for the innocent Israelis blown apart by suicide bombers, and the Palestinian children killed by retaliatory strikes that missed their mark. Heavy for the victims of murder and kidnapping; for the children who were molested by priests who betrayed our trust; and for those innocent priests whose lives have been destroyed by false allegations. These are some of the signs of dismay that I see in the sun, the moon, the stars, and on our earth.

But Jesus is speaking to us about times like these in today's Gospel. He is telling us to take care that our hearts do not become overwhelmed by the bad things that happen around us. As disciples of Jesus in the 21st century we must have both of our feet firmly planted in reality — that reality, unfortunately, is that the world has an abundance of evil and suffering. But as true disciples of Jesus, we must never lose faith in the power of goodness and love, and the potential for redemption.

Jesus calls us to be agents of that redemption. He calls us to bear witness by our actions that the love of God can indeed flow into the world through ordinary people like you and me. He calls us not to just balance out the evil and suffering in the world, but to transform and redeem it.

This is the first Sunday in Advent and it is also the first day of a new Church year of life. It is a good time for us to recommit ourselves to live out our Christian faith in such a way that each of us is a beacon of God's light and love.

Two thousand years ago Jesus was born into a world filled with evil and suffering. As we prepare ourselves to celebrate his birthday, let us remember that we, as his disciples, are part of his unfinished mission. And let us renew our hearts to be true to that mission — to bring God's light and his love into the darkest most dismal corners of our world.

November 2003
Advent

The Greatest Role Model

John 13: 4 – 5, 12 - 14

(Jesus) got up from supper, and laid aside his garments; and taking a towel, he girded himself. Then he poured water into the basin, and began to wash the disciples' feet and to wipe them with the towel . . . So when he had washed their feet, and taken his garments and reclined at the table again, he said to them, "Do you know what I have done to you? You call me Teacher and Lord; and you are right, for so I am. If I then, the Lord and the Teacher, washed your feet, you also ought to wash one another's feet."

*

There is a special kind of service that comes from the heart. The ancient Greeks had a word for it, *diakonia*. It is the root of the English adjective *diaconal* and the noun *deacon*. We Christians are called to be a *diaconal* people: a people in loving service to God and to our neighbor.

The role model for deacons and for all baptized Christians is the Servant Christ. Jesus, as he is depicted in tonight's Gospel, sets the example of how we are called to live our lives. At the end of that Gospel, after he has washed the feet of his friends, Jesus tells them that he has given them a model to follow: *"If I then, the Lord and the Teacher, washed your feet, you also ought to wash one another's feet."* It's not just the symbolic act of washing the feet of another; it's not just the act of serving; it is that very special service that comes from the heart — *diakonia* — to which we are called.

Real *diakonia*, genuine loving service, needs to be freely given to everyone. Not just our loved ones but to those who have hurt us deeply; to those who act and live in ways we find hard to understand; even to those who have turned away from God and from human goodness.

This is what sets Christianity apart from other religions and philosophies: If we love those who love us, what great thing is that? But if we love, genuinely love, those who hurt us, that is the real deal. And Jesus is the realest deal that ever was or ever will be.

We all know the Gospel story we heard tonight; we all have the image of Jesus washing the feet of the apostles. What many people miss, however, is the presence of Judas, the person who hurt and betrayed Jesus. Judas is not excluded — his feet are washed by Jesus with the same loving service he extends to the others.

As Lent comes to an end, as we prepare to meet the Risen Christ, let us examine our lives, and let us reach out — like Jesus — with forgiveness and loving service to those who have hurt us, even if it's not reciprocated. He has given us a model to follow: *"If I then, the Lord and the Teacher, washed your feet, you also ought to wash one another's feet."*

Perhaps, the greatest Lenten gift we can offer to God will be to go home, pick up the phone, and reopen the doors and the windows of our hearts.

April 2004
Holy Thursday

<u>*One Thing*</u>

Mark 12: 28-34

One of the scribes came and heard them arguing, and recognizing that he had answered them well, asked him, "What commandment is the foremost of all?" Jesus answered, "The foremost is, 'Hear, O Israel! The Lord our God is one Lord; and you shall love the Lord your God with all your heart, and with all your soul, and with all your mind, and with all your strength.' The second is this, 'You shall love your neighbor as yourself.' There is no other commandment greater than these." The scribe said to him, "Right, Teacher; you have truly stated that he is one, and there is no one else beside him; and to love him with all the heart and with all the understanding and with all the strength, and to love one's neighbor as himself, is much more than all burnt offerings and sacrifices." When Jesus saw that he had answered intelligently, he said to him, "You are not far from the kingdom of God."

*

Do you know what the secret of life is? It's this.

One thing. You stick to that *one thing* and nothing else really matters.

It takes a lot of faith for some of us to keep coming here week after week. Every day we hear about unexplainable evil and suffering somewhere in the world. Personal tragedy sometimes even hits our own lives. Sometimes we suffer a great, deep hurt from someone we loved and trusted; from someone or something we believed in, maybe even dedicated our life to. Some of us may be hurt or disappointed by decisions made by the hierarchy of our Church. And yet we keep coming, week after week, season after season, year after year. Where does this kind of faith come from?

Faith is a gift but we have to accept it. It's a big gift and if we try to reach for it with one hand, it's going to be shaky. We need to embrace this gift with both arms open wide to take it fully. We need to embrace it with our whole heart, our whole soul, and our whole mind. This means that our personal relationship with God becomes the center and most important part of our lives.

I saw a movie about three years ago called *City Slickers*. It stars Billy Crystal and Jack Palance. Jack Palance received an Oscar for his performance. In the movie Billy Crystal is a burnt-out business executive going through a mid-life crisis, a depression. Job, family, friends have all lost their meaning for him. There is no more joy in life. He goes out West to a dude ranch to participate in a two week cattle drive hoping to find himself.

Jack Palance is the tough trail boss named Curly. Curly is a seasoned, no nonsense cowboy who has spent his whole life herding cattle. Curly sees how depressed Billy Crystal is, and asks him, "Do you know what the secret of life is? It's this," and he raises up one finger. "One thing." Curly tells him, "You stick to that one thing and nothing else matters."

"What's the one thing?" Billy Crystal asks. Curly answers, "That's for you to figure out."

Two thousand years ago, someone asked Jesus what that one thing was. We heard the story in today's Gospel: *"What is the foremost commandment of all?"* [What is the secret of life?] And Jesus answered, one thing ". . . *you shall love the Lord your God with all your heart, and with all your soul, and with all your mind, and with all your strength . . . (and) you shall love your neighbor as yourself."*

When we embrace that *one thing,* we are making God the center and most important part of our life. We are reaching with both arms to accept the amazing gift of faith.

That faith will carry us through all the pain and hurt, all the confusion and struggle of our own lives. It will give us the strength to live in a world that all too often seems filled with evil and suffering. It will give us the hope and the courage to never give up; to keep trying to build God's kingdom here among us — a kingdom of love and compassion; a kingdom of justice and equality.

It is faith that enables us to open ourselves totally to God; to make God the center of our existence; to love God with our whole heart, and our whole soul, and our whole mind, and to love our neighbor as ourselves.

This is the secret of life — *one thing.*

Once we find that one thing, nothing else really matters.

October 1994
Ordinary Time

Prayer

Luke 18: 1

(Jesus) was telling them a parable to show that at all times they ought to pray and not to lose heart.

*

Jesus told his friends to pray always and not lose heart. But what is prayer all about? Can we really change God's mind or his will by our prayers? I don't think so. But we can indeed change the course of events with prayer. Because prayer doesn't change God, it changes us — it makes us into new persons with new options for the future.

When I was a young Catholic school boy back in the Bronx, prayer was a simple matter. I just made the nine first Fridays and I was guaranteed a seat in heaven. All I had to do to pass my math test was to neatly etch the initials of Jesus, Mary and Joseph, *JMJ*, on the top of my test paper. But of course that was before Vatican II.

As I grew into a young man of the 1960s, I became intellectually uncomfortable with the concept of prayer. I developed a distorted view of prayer as a self serving attempt to manipulate God — something that I was way above trying; unless, of course, I lost my car keys when, after holding out for a mere 45 seconds, I'd be begging Saint Anthony to find them — and he always did! I never could figure how those keys would magically reappear. And, you know, they still do.

As I've matured in my faith, I have come to understand that prayer is not about changing God, but about changing the person who prays. Prayer is about letting go. It's about emptying ourselves, so that there is room for God to come into our hearts to change US.

We are filled with clutter: anxieties and agendas and instructions for God. So filled, that there is no room for God to get in. Before God can work within us, we need to let go, to empty ourselves of all the clutter.

It's not so easy to empty ourselves, to let go of all that clutter. There is so much clutter in our world — things to fill us with anxiety and dread. But it can be done. Each of us has to find our own way.

Dag Hammarskjold was Secretary General of the UN in the 1950s and early 1960s. His job caused him to witness the dark side of human nature, over and over again: violence, war, bloodshed, greed, political betrayal. You could say he had a front row view of original sin.

And yet Dag Hammarskjold remained a man of faith, a deeply spiritual human being. Perhaps he is best remembered by the answer he gave when asked by a reporter what he said to God when he prayed. Hammarskjold responded, "For everything that has gone before, thank you! For everything that is still to come, yes!"

Three little words, 'thank you' and 'yes'; that's how Dag Hammarskjold emptied himself to make room for God. Each of us has to find our own way.

September 1994
Ordinary Time

The Christ Child Within

Mark 9: 36 – 37

Taking a child, (Jesus) set him before them, and taking him in his arms, he said to them, "Whoever receives one child like this in my name receives me; and whoever receives me does not receive me, but him who sent me."

*

"When you welcome the child, you are really welcoming me." Who is this magical child and why does he try to force himself into our lives?

Deep within each of us is a little child. This little child is the real *me* — put there by God to know him, love him, serve him, and to be happy with him for all eternity. But who is this real *me*? Is it the personal 'me' that we see when we look in the mirror: the 'me' that was born on such and such a date, travels through life with a history of joys and sorrows, relationships and losses, successes and failures, and will eventually die on such and such a date? Or is it that timeless *me* at the center of our being, our immortal soul, the Christ-child within us?

Thanks to psychology, we have learned much about the 'little child' within us, and the need to set that child free — free from the wounds of any early trauma that might prevent it from living and loving life to its fullest. This is the personal 'me' within the human psyche. But we also have within us another child, a child that longs to be set free from the prison of personal selfishness; that longs to love with all of its being. This is the real *me* — this is the Christ-child within.

Through the Gospel, Jesus calls us to be free. Like a butterfly emerging from its cocoon, we are called to let go of that personal child — that 'me', and to welcome into our midst and embrace the Christ-child within us.

But to properly welcome that child, we must first clean out our closets. Unfortunately, our closets are often filled with baggage — emotional baggage collected over a lifetime: anger, hurt, resentment and self-alienation.

Buried away, behind all that baggage is our Christ child, our ticket home to God. And like the little child in today's Gospel, the child that Jesus embraced and brought into the midst of his disciples, the Christ-child within the closet of our soul can be easily missed — drowned out and obscured by the noise of the world.

What stands in our way? What makes it so tough for us to find and welcome that Christ-child? Life can be difficult. Things happen. Life happens. We sometimes get hurt — wounded very deeply. We accumulate history, and with that history comes the baggage, emotional baggage. Little by little that Christ-child within our soul gets pushed to the back of the closet.

To find and welcome that child, we must open the closet of our mind, and one by one get rid of all that baggage we no longer need — the baggage that has buried the child. Packed away within that baggage for some of us are painful, unresolved feelings towards others: the memory of physical, emotional or sexual abuse; the pain of abandonment as a child by a parent we may have lost through divorce, death or a debilitating addiction or illness; the hurt of betrayal as an adult by someone we loved and trusted very deeply; anger towards God for an illness or handicap we are struggling through life with; or for taking someone from us in death. The list goes on and on. And yet, Jesus tells us to get rid of the baggage and to welcome the child.

Some of us have baggage filled with self-alienation, self-hatred: for not being perfect; for not being someone, anyone, other than who we are; for something awful we may have done along the way, for which God has long since forgiven us, even though we can't seem to forgive ourselves. And yet Jesus asks us to get rid of the baggage and to welcome the child.

This baggage is hard to let go of. It is usually the result of some very real hurt and damage we have experienced in life. But if we hold on to the anger, the hurt, the resentment, the self-alienation, it becomes like a blockage in the artery of God's love. It stands in the way of our being able to love God, to love each other and to love ourselves. It keeps us locked in a prison of bitterness, anxiety, and depression and makes it difficult for God's love to flow through us and into the world. It makes it real tough for us to welcome the Christ-child into our midst.

But Jesus never gives up. He keeps calling to us from way behind all the baggage of our lives. His gentle, reassuring voice asks us to let that wounded child within our mind be touched by the magic of God's unconditional love. He whispers to us in the flowers, in the song of a morning bird, in the smile of a friend. He's there with the promise of hope as we open our eyes on each new day, each new beginning to the rest of our journey.

He asks us to let go of the past, of the anger, of the hurt, of the fear; to forgive; to be loved and to love unconditionally, without strings.

That Christ-child within will never give up. He's calling to us now. He's calling us to hug him and bring him into the center of our life. He's calling us to be healed. He's calling us to be whole.

October 1993
Ordinary Time

The Last Supper Table

Mark 14: 22 -24

While they were eating, he took some bread, and after a blessing he broke it, and gave it to them, and said, "Take it; this is my body." And when he had taken a cup and given thanks, he gave it to them, and they all drank from it. And he said to them, "This is my blood of the covenant."

*

Some of the happiest times that I can remember in my life were spent around a dinner table. There is something so wonderful about sharing a meal with people I love — the warmth, the laughter, the lively discussion. This is community at its best; it is communion; it is a gift. The Last Supper was such a gift. And Jesus was able to extend that Last Supper table horizontally to all people in all cultures and vertically throughout the ages. He created the greatest communion and drew us all into one timeless moment. He gave us the gift of himself in the Eucharist.

When we come here to the Lord's table we are stepping through a portal in time. We are still in Tenafly, but at the same time we are back at that dinner table in Jerusalem. We are sharing the laughter, the warmth, the lively discussion with Jesus and his friends.

We are also sharing in the mystery of Redemption: the life, death and resurrection of our God. Our God who stepped into time to become flesh and blood like us; to ride the bus of life with us; to laugh, to love, to suffer and die with us.

What happens here is not just symbolic. When the priest says the words, "This is My Body," past, present and future come together and Christ's loving, redemptive work happens again in real time. At that moment we are at the Last Supper table, we are at the foot of the cross; we are at the empty tomb.

It is a privilege for me to stand here each Sunday and give you Holy Communion. When I look into your eyes and say the words, "The Body of Christ," time and space stand still. What a joy to be present as you embrace Our Lord and he embraces you.

Let us be thankful for that dinner that started back in Jerusalem and is still being served. Let us be thankful for having been invited. And let us thank God for the gift of the Eucharist, the Body and Blood of Christ.

June 2009
Feast of the Body and Blood of Christ

Our Blessed Mother

All my life I have had a deep devotion to Mary. She is known by many names: from the Blessed Mother, to the Holy Virgin, to Our Lady Queen of the Sea, to Our Lady of Mount Carmel. But regardless of the name or the culture or the parish, Mary touches something very deep within the human psyche.

Historically she was a young Jewish teenager who said 'yes' to God's call. She nurtured Jesus into adulthood and lived a life of loving service right up to the very end. It was not an easy life.

Mary suffered great personal losses from the disappearance of twelve year old Jesus during a trip to Jerusalem, to the early death of her husband, to the witnessing of her son's brutal execution. But through all these events, Mary kept her heart wide open to God's love and she let that love flow through her to everyone she interacted with — everyone — from her extended family, to the apostles and disciples, to the occupying Roman forces, and to each and every one of us who has ever turned to her in prayer for help.

Our Blessed Mother was human. She was flesh and blood like us. With all the suffering and the loss that she endured, she had to feel grief and anger; she had to question God at times in the face of such sorrow.

What made Mary so special was that she never, not for one instant, allowed her heart to close down, allowed herself to turn inward and fall into the abyss of self pity or rage. Mary never turned away from other people. She never turns away from us.

Mary experienced loss and abandonment and betrayal like many of us. She could have caved in to depression; she could have allowed anxiety to cripple her. But she didn't. She lived each day in loving service to all those around her.

This young Jewish girl who became a blessed mother to all of us is our role model. Each of us is called to live our lives like Mary lived hers — to keep saying 'yes' to God's call; a call we receive every morning when we open our eyes on each new day, each new beginning.

Each of us is called to deal with the inescapable sufferings of life: the hurts, the disappointments, the losses, and the emotional and physical pain, like Mary. She could have allowed herself to give in to anger — to go through life with rage over what was done to her son. But she didn't. She chose life, she chose love.

> *Holy Mary, Mother of God, Our Lady of Mount Carmel, pray for us who struggle.*
> *Fill our hearts with your strength, with your loving nature.*
> *Help us to choose to live our lives as you chose to live yours — without anger, without bitterness or self-pity.*
> *Help us to live each day in loving service to God, to our family and to all those with whom we interact.*

July 2002
Feast of Our Lady of Mount Carmel

This Moment

Luke 12: 16 – 21

(Jesus) told them a parable, saying, "The land of a rich man was very productive. And he began reasoning to himself, saying, 'What shall I do, since I have no place to store my crops?' Then he said, 'This is what I will do: I will tear down my barns and build larger ones, and there I will store all my grain and my goods. And I will say to my soul, "Soul, you have many goods laid up for many years to come; take your ease, eat, drink and be merry."' But God said to him, 'You fool! This very night your soul is required of you; and now who will own what you have prepared?' So is the man who stores up treasure for himself, and is not rich toward God."

*

A moment is all that is guaranteed to any one of us. And that moment is now; this moment. The past is gone; it lives on only in our memories. Our future here on earth may or may never happen.

Our life is a tapestry of moments sewn together in a pattern created over time. This pattern gets shaped day by day by the treasures that we store up within our hearts. In the end it could be a pattern that reflects the material possessions, credentials and honors that we have accumulated. Or it could be a pattern that reflects acts of love: love of God, and love of others.

Like the man in today's Gospel, our lives could be demanded from us this day, this night. And if our soul were to be taken up by God, and if we were to stand side by side with him and look down at the tapestry of the life we have lived, what pattern, what treasures would we see?

We would see a pattern that reflects how well we loved God and treated others. Were we loving and caring, or bitter and angry? Were we kind and forgiving, or did we carry a grudge? Were we inclusive, non-judgmental and accepting, or did we shut people out of our lives because they were different or didn't measure up to our moral standards? Were there family members and friends whom we locked out of our hearts because of some real or imagined slight that we can't even remember?

Each day, each moment of life that God gives us is precious. But in any one of those moments our earthly life can suddenly come to an end. If that moment were to come today what unfinished business would we leave behind? Death leaves us no chance to say "Goodbye," no chance to say "I'm sorry," no chance to say "I forgive you."

Let us not be like the rich man in today's Gospel. Rather than being concerned about building larger barns to store our possessions, let us be rich in what matters to God. Let us examine our lives and reach out with contrition where needed, and with forgiveness to those who have hurt us. Let us be instruments of healing in all the circles of our lives. Let us love and serve the Lord by loving and serving each other.

A moment is all that is guaranteed to any one of us. And that moment is now.

August 2010
Ordinary Time

Mary's 'Yes'

There's a great anticipation throughout the world surrounding the arrival of Y2K. I can't help but wonder what the world thought about back when Y0K was approaching. Today, in 1999, there is anxiety that borders on hysteria — anxiety that the world as we know it will never be the same again. But there is also, in the midst of a material and self-centered world, a deep yearning for spirituality.

Such was the case back in Y0K when a young teenage girl was visited by an angel and given an amazing invitation — an invitation to be the mother of the Word of God made flesh; to be the instrument for changing the world forever. And Mary accepted.

But it could have been different. I think that the wonder, the blessedness of Mary is that she had the freedom to say 'no' to God but chose to say 'yes'. And in so doing she allowed her body and every single talent that she had to be used for the glory of God, and to ease the suffering of the human race.

The Church teaches us that even as Mary was being conceived in her mother's womb, God knew that she would lead a life of total goodness; and that at every decision point she would come to in life, Mary would always choose to say 'yes' to God's love. And because God knew all of this he gave Mary a very special grace at her conception. Basically, God told the angels that this little girl, this immaculate human soul would always chose light rather than darkness; and because of her unselfishness, the world would come to hear the Word of God.

Because of Mary's willingness to say 'yes' back in Y0K, we as citizens of Y2K have the Word of God present to us in the Gospel, and in the Eucharist. And that Word of God is constantly inviting us, like Mary, to say 'yes'; to use the gift of our lives and our talents for the glory of God and to ease the suffering of the human race.

So let us greet Y2K like Mary greeted that Angel. Let us see in the challenges of our personal lives, and in our work a call to follow in Mary's footsteps; an invitation to consecrate every act of ours from the simple task of washing a dish to the intricacies of caring for one who is dying; an invitation to make the Word of God present in our corner of the world; an invitation to say 'yes' to God's love.

December 1999
Feast of the Immaculate Conception

Healing

Matthew 17: 20

(Jesus said to them), ". . . if you have faith the size of a mustard seed, you will say to this mountain, 'Move from here to there,' and it will move; and nothing will be impossible to you."

*

When I was a young child, I listened to the Gospel stories with awe. To me, Jesus was the greatest superhero of all time. Forget about Superman or the Green Hornet. Like I would argue with my fourth grade friends, "When did Batman ever heal a leper or restore sight to a blind man?"

I fantasized about how wonderful it must have been for Jesus to heal people who were so desperately ill. I wished that I could be like him and give people back their health. I remember seeing a one-legged man struggling along on crutches under the Third Avenue El in the Bronx and feeling so badly for him. In my 10 year old mind, I wished that I could be like Jesus and just hold out my hand, pray to the Father and give that man back his missing leg.

But as I matured in my faith I came to understand that Jesus' ministry was about healing illness and not just about curing disease. There is a distinction between an illness and a disease: human beings suffer illnesses, physicians diagnose and treat diseases.

A person suffering from an illness, let's take leprosy for example, not only suffers from the physical symptoms of the disease; that person also may experience a sense of loss of his or her value to society and a loss of self-worth.

This sense of loss is reinforced by societies that divide the world into the 'clean' and the 'unclean', the righteous and the sinner, the good and the bad. This can lead to alienation from one's self, and even to alienation from God. Because it's hard to accept that God loves you when society has thrown you into the dumpster and you have learned to hate yourself.

In Palestinian society at the time of Jesus' ministry, a person with leprosy was not a threat to society because of medical infection or epidemic. The leper was more of a threat because of symbolic contamination. Obviously, the leper was a leper because he or she had done something to deserve it. And to hang around with lepers, even to minister to lepers, meant not only that you might catch it, but that maybe you too were a bad person deserving to be shut out and forgotten by society.

So what was Jesus doing in his healing miracles? Was he only curing the disease through some supernatural intervention in the physical world, or was he also healing the illness through an intervention in the social world — changing the hearts and minds of people by cutting through their prejudice?

Not only did Jesus reach out to and love human beings whom society had discarded, but by refusing to accept their status as outcasts, he in effect turned back to that society and challenged it to either reject him from the community or to accept the outcast within it as well. Jesus still poses that challenge. And by virtue of that challenge he invites us as his disciples, his Church, to follow in his footsteps and to be miracle workers and healers to all our sisters and brothers.

Every age and every culture has its form of leprosy. Moving from Palestine of the first century to New Jersey in the late 20th century, we have a new leprosy called AIDS. What started out as a handful of cases in 1981 has mushroomed to nearly 350,000 reported cases in the United States. At the end of 1993 the total was almost 20,000 in New Jersey alone; and over 60% of the people who suffer from AIDS in the state of New Jersey live within the four counties of our Archdiocese of Newark. The cases are divided evenly among men, women and children. This statement bears repeating — the cases are divided evenly among men, women and children.

In all communities, whether urban or suburban, impoverished or affluent, heterosexual or homosexual, the tragedy of AIDS continues to strike. Although we have heard and read much regarding AIDS, there are still many people who continue to suffer in shame and isolation — abandoned by their families and rejected by friends and neighbors. For some, there is no one to care and nowhere to go. For others their hearts break a little more each day as they care for a loved one who is painfully dying.

Individually as disciples of Jesus, and collectively as his Church, we are called to respond to this tragedy with compassion and love. The bishops of the United States have written a Pastoral Letter concerning AIDS. I would like to share part of this letter with you.

> *"Persons with AIDS must not become occasions for stereotyping or prejudice, for anger or recrimination, for rejection or isolation, for injustice or condemnation. They provide us with an opportunity to walk with those who are suffering, to be compassionate toward those whom we might otherwise fear, to bring strength and courage both to those who face the prospect of dying as well as their loved ones."*

Our own Archbishop Theodore McCarrick has designated today, June 12th, as AIDS Compassion Sunday in the Archdiocese of Newark. I would like to share an excerpt from Archbishop McCarrick's letter to all parishes:

"Our Church will always respond with compassion to the needs of God's children in time of crisis. It is for this reason that I designate Sunday, June 12, as AIDS Compassion Sunday. Because of this observance over the past few years, families affected by this tragedy have identified more with their faith as a source of comfort and hope . By nurturing this faith in those who are in such desperate need for hope in their lives, we are reminded of the comfort and support we have each received from our Savior in our own time of personal need."

Our archdiocese operates several ministries to people with AIDS and their loved ones. Among the programs and services offered are: volunteers who visit with and share one-on-one time with people with AIDS living in hospices and residences around the diocese; volunteers who cook and deliver meals to a residence for people with AIDS on the grounds of Bergen Pines Hospital; volunteers who arrange and provide transportation for people with AIDS; support groups for people with AIDS and for people who are caring for a loved one who suffers with

AIDS; walk-in services and referrals for people with AIDS, which include meals, emergency supplies of food, clothing and small appliances.

If anyone is in need of these services for either themselves or for a loved one, or would like to consider the possibility of volunteering to minister in any of these areas, please contact me, in confidence, either after Mass or through the rectory.

God calls each of us to have faith like a mustard seed, but he's counting on us not to stop there. He calls us to be instruments of his unconditional love, compassion and acceptance; to minister to his children wherever the need is greatest.

We are called not to be some comic book superhero like Batman, but to be healers and lovers like the greatest real live, flesh and blood hero the world has ever known — Jesus of Nazareth.

June 1994
Ordinary Time

Bloom Where You Are Planted

Matthew 4: 19 – 20

(Jesus) said to them, "Follow me, and I will make you fishers of men." Immediately they left their nets and followed him.

*

When those fishermen in today's Gospel looked up and heard Jesus call to them, they felt this overpowering, unconditional love. That love was so strong that they dropped their nets, climbed out of their boats and went running after him.

When we hear this Gospel story it's exciting and inspiring; but there is something behind the story that's even more relevant and important for us. Even though these fishermen dropped what they were doing, followed Jesus and eventually became great saints, they still went back to work the next day. Those who had families still went home to eat supper with their wives and play with their kids.

We know this from later Gospel stories that put them back in their boats hauling fish or caring for sick in-laws. We even have a story where they brought Jesus along with them in the boat. The point of the story is this: once these ordinary fishermen said 'yes' to Jesus, their ordinary lives were changed forever.

When I was a child and heard today's Gospel, I wanted to be like those fishermen and follow Jesus. But I thought that meant dropping everything in my life, leaving every relationship behind. As an adult I came to understand that we are called to follow Jesus within the circles and relationships of our own lives; we are all called to be builders of the Kingdom of God no matter what else we might happen to be doing.

We don't have to leave our world behind to follow that unconditional love. We can follow and embrace Jesus by unconditionally loving others. By so doing, we can make Jesus present in the circumstances and circles of our lives. It's like bringing Jesus along in the boat as we do our work.

There's an old saying, "Bloom where you are planted." God has planted each of us somewhere in the garden of time and space. We are rich, poor, single, or married. Some of us are construction workers, executives, doctors, homemakers, priests and any of a thousand other profiles. But each of us has heard Jesus' call to follow him or we wouldn't be here in this room today.

So here we are 2,000 years later in our own fishing boats in Tenafly, New Jersey; and Jesus is still out there standing on the shore, calling us to follow. Whatever the circumstances of our lives, whatever our individual roles and responsibilities, he calls us to be loving and forgiving, gentle and kind; to be a healing force for our world; to be fishers of men and women for the Kingdom of God — and that Kingdom begins right here on earth.

January 2009
Ordinary Time

Postscript

Credo

O Lord, you have searched me and known me.
. . . You formed my inward parts;
You wove me in my mother's womb.
I will give thanks to you, for I am . . . wonderfully made;
Wonderful are your works,
and my soul knows it very well.

Psalm 139: 1-2, 13-14

*

When God made me and you he embraced each of us like a mother would bundle up a beloved child to go out into the cold for the very first time. And like a parent might slip a little identification note into a child's pocket, just in case he or she should get lost, God put a little piece of himself inside of us.

That little piece of God inside of every human being is our immortal soul, and life is the journey of our soul back home to its loving creator. We are created for that journey with free will by a loving God, the source of all goodness and love; a God who came into our time and space to rescue us from our mistakes and to redeem us by example, by showing us the way to get home. God sanctifies us, over and over again, with sufficient grace to transform ourselves into instruments of God's love, and to help bring about his Kingdom in the now and forever.

God gave us the freedom to return or reject his love. We return that love by genuinely loving God, others and ourselves; that's how love goes back to Love; that's how our souls go back to God. We reject that love when we sin — when we fail to love God, others and ourselves.

When we sin, we turn away from God. But God doesn't go away; neither does he patiently stand there waiting in the wings. God passionately pursues us. Just like a loving parent is ready to risk and sacrifice his or her life to save a child, God did that for us.

Through the Incarnation God took human form and came into our world to show us, by example, how to get home. By so doing God redeemed us at great price: sharing in our suffering, in the effects of humanity's sin.

The Paschal Mystery, God's redeeming act in history on Calvary and every day in the Eucharist, is like a flashlight in the darkness of sin and selfishness. This 'flashlight' points the way to our salvation, our personal transformation away from sin and selfishness and back to love, to God. But to be transformed we must say 'yes', we must choose to turn back. The gift of free will is the option to say 'yes' or 'no'. When we choose 'yes' we are sanctified, and because we made that choice, because we said 'yes,' we receive the grace to turn back, as many times as necessary, until the relationship is restored, and ultimately we are home with God.

'God' is a word that we humans use to define an indefinable reality. Because our minds and bodies operate in time and space, we are comfortable thinking and speaking with intellectual constructs. We anthropomorphize our Creator. We paint pictures, cut stained-glass images, and sing songs about a reality that cannot be packaged into the limited box of human understanding. What the intellect struggles to grasp, the soul already knows. I intuitively know that there is a central, loving, and personal source of all creation. I know this because God embraced me before I was born. I use the word 'God' but the concept goes beyond language, beyond culture and religion; it goes to the depth of my soul.

God is love. Carole King wrote a song in the 1970s, *Only Love is Real, Everything Else An Illusion.* For me this song speaks of God. Saint John preached that "God is Love." So 'God' and 'Love' have the same meaning. Whether we call it 'The Force', 'The Tao', 'God', 'Nature', 'Love', it's the same. And whether we believe that God knows us intellectually with a mind that uses language and constructs like the human mind, or that he knows us in some other way that is beyond the limits of human comprehension — God still *knows* and *loves* each and every one of us.

God is pure love. It's hard to grasp this concept so we Christians use an intellectual construct in attempting to describe the dynamic of that pure Love. The construct is Trinity. In my first year systematic theology course, I was introduced to Kilian McDonnell's analogical model of the *Trinitarian cycle of life.* Father McDonnell uses this construct to speak about the underlying Trinitarian dynamic: "this dynamic is God reaching through the Son in the Spirit to touch and transform the world and the church to lead them in the Spirit through the Son back to God." In this model the energy flows from *source* (God) through *conduit* (God) and back to *goal* (God). The analogy defines source as Father, conduits as Son and Spirit, and goal as Father. McDonnell writes that it is within this flow of energy, this "dynamic of life from the Father to the Father" that we find "the extension of

Trinitarian life beyond the divine self to cosmos and church in the missions of the Son and the Spirit." This imagery helps me to grasp the dynamic of love that forms the essence of God.

Resonating even more deeply for me is Meister Eckhart's image of the Trinity: "When God laughs at the soul and the soul laughs back at God, the persons of the Trinity are begotten. To speak in hyperbole, when the Father laughs at the Son and the Son laughs back at the Father, that laughter gives pleasure, that pleasure gives joy, that joy gives love, and that love gives the persons [of the Trinity] of which the Holy Spirit is one." The indefinable reality of God is brought within the fringes of my intellectual and emotional grasp with the image of a Triune God who is love. This reality, *God*, is the source of all goodness and love and the bedrock of my belief; it is the first and foremost central doctrine of my faith.

McDonnell and Eckhart and novice theologians like myself, would never be in touch with the reality of God had we not been redeemed. *Redemption* is humanity's defining moment. Susan Windley-Daoust defines the connection between the soul's ability to know God and God's redeeming act on our behalf: "To speak of how we know God is to speak of an experience of redemption that is beyond our linguistic capabilities: at best we capture fragments of this wholly Other with whom we are in relationship. Yet the existence of the redemptive relationship at all enables and calls us to tell others, to express the defining moment of our lives." But why did we need this defining moment at all? Why did we need redemption? The answer is one word, sin.

As a young Catholic school boy back in the Bronx I learned all about original sin from the good sisters. This ominous sounding condition was a black mark on my soul that I inherited from Adam and Eve through no fault of my own; and only the waters of Baptism could wash it away. This whole concept bothered me: I mean, after all, what did I have to do with Adam and Eve? I didn't even like apples. But those days back in the Bronx were a long time ago, long before I came to know how I, how we, can hurt others and ourselves by turning away from God's love. As a mature human being who strives to become Christian, I came to understand original sin to be the basic, inherent human tendency to be self-centered and selfish; to put my interests, needs and survival before the love of God and the needs of others; to turn inward rather than reach outward, in love with God and with my neighbor.

Taken to its extreme, original sin can be deadly to us, our families and to society. While we focus on ourselves and our own needs, it's difficult for God's unconditional love to flow through us into a world very much in need of that love. While we focus on ourselves, it's hard to hear God calling to us in the song of a morning bird, the patter of a summer night's rain; to see God in the eyes of our children, in the smile of our lover. While we focus on ourselves, it's difficult to hear the cries of the lonely, the desperation of the oppressed, and the hunger of the poor. While we focus on ourselves, not only do we miss the chance to love and to reach out to others, but we run the risk of becoming so self-absorbed that we, like Narcissus, drown in our own reflection.

Perhaps God knew that if he endowed humans with free will some would make really bad choices, and sin would enter the world. But God took the risk; the first human children of God were loved enough to be set free. And God, the loving parent, waited for them to come home. Unfortunately, something else happened; there were acts of selfishness and destruction. But God didn't want to take away the gift of freedom. It was really important to God that we journey through life and learn to freely love and, ultimately, choose to come home to spend eternity with him. So God, in his boundless love for me and you and everyone, made a leap of faith — in us, and took another risk. Just as a loving parent is ready to sacrifice his or her life to save a child, God did that for us. God was incarnated and took fully human form in the person of Jesus of Nazareth, the Christ. Jesus was like us in all things except sin; how could he sin, he is pure love, he is God. He was born into our time and space and came into our world to show us, by his example, how to love and how to get home. Through this great act of love, in the person of Jesus, God redeemed us.

In redeeming us, Jesus set the example of how we are called to live, and grow, and love, and die to self so that we can be born to eternal life. Jesus' mission wasn't to suffer and die to appease God. His mission was to show us the way, the example, by proclaiming the Kingdom of God; and to call us to action to make that Kingdom a reality. Jesus didn't have to die on the cross. His death was the result of the fundamental way in which he lived: he preached the unconditional love of the Father, and God's call to us to love others in the same way; as a result he collided with people and interest groups that thought they had the way to God all figured out. He died because he chose to continue his mission despite the consequences, consequences from a self-righteous and self-centered world that wasn't ready to buy what Jesus was selling.

Jesus died because he chose to make the ultimate sacrifice for us, God's children. He willingly accepted the consequences of setting the example for us, and of proclaiming God's radical message of unconditional love. Through the Gospel he still proclaims that message today 2,000 years later. The cross, the nails, the thorns couldn't stop him.

Just as Jesus gave us the moral model to influence how we choose to live, he calls us to morally influence others by our lives. He asks us to continue his mission; to let each of our lives be a homily, a sermon, a living proclamation of the Kingdom of God; to preach that Kingdom by the way we love, forgive and accept each other unconditionally; to live our lives as such reflections of his message that long after we're gone people will say that through us the mission of Jesus goes on.

Alongside the gift of example, of moral influence for humanity, the redemption and its symbolization in the cross is also an answer to the problem of evil. Sometimes life doesn't make sense; there is chaos, there is darkness; bad things happen. Sometimes, no matter how good we are, how loving; no matter how hard we try, we cannot escape the pain and contradictions of human existence; we cannot escape the consequences of sin. The symbol of our redemption is itself a contradiction — the cross, two opposing beams of wood made from the tree of life, used to torture and destroy life — and in the center of the contradiction we find God in human form. But the message of the cross is hope. It tells us that we are not alone, that God is with us in the chaos and the darkness; that he is present in the pain, loss and disillusionment; that he is holding our hand through the suffering. It tells us that God is there at the center of the chaos and contradiction, at the center of the cross. And if we follow the example set by God's redemption, someday, once we are free of the constraints of human existence and the limitations of human understanding, it will all make sense; there will be a happy ending — or more truly, a happy beginning of eternity with God. *Redemption* — God's great leap of faith and risk to save us by example and teach us how to love — is the second central doctrine of my faith.

Whereas God, in the person of Jesus, redeemed us by showing the way to get home; God, in the person of the Holy Spirit, *sanctifies* and transforms us, over and over again throughout our life journey, with grace. This grace is sufficient, when we are faced with issues of selfishness, suffering, and sin, to help us keep walking through the darkness towards the light. Redemption notwithstanding, God still takes a leap of faith in us; even after Calvary, he did not withdraw his gift of free will. The gift of free will is the choice to say 'yes' or 'no' to God's love. Each time we choose 'yes' we are sanctified; and because we made that choice, because we said 'yes,' the Holy Spirit strengthens us and we receive the grace to transform, to follow through on our resolve for goodness.

Sanctification brings grace that transforms us, and grace is the sustenance of God's Kingdom. Grace helps us to open our hearts and accept God's love, and to let that love transform us so that we can transform the world. With the action of the Holy Spirit we open ourselves to become channels of God's unconditional love. Each time we choose to respond 'yes' to God, there is a sanctifying act of transformation within us. The Kingdom of God is a series of acts of personal transformation. All those acts of transformation, past, present, and future make a mosaic which is, was and will be the Kingdom of God.

Grace helps us remember how much we are loved by God. Once we are touched by that love it is the most natural thing to want to follow God to the ends of the earth. There's a song by Christopher Walker often played at Communion time in my parish that always brings this to mind: "Lord, you are my shepherd, you are my friend, I want to follow you always, just to follow my friend." My life has been filled with God's grace and I have felt the Lord's Presence walking with me as my friend; that is why I wanted to follow him as a deacon. At the heights and in the pits; when I have felt joy and surrounded by love, and when I was depressed and lost in the universe — the Lord was always there with me. Many times my back was to the wall and it seemed that there was no way out; yet, God always made a window in the wall and pulled me through. I want to follow him always, just to follow my friend.

Sanctified with grace by the Holy Spirit, we can be God's human hands in this world; channels of his love enabling that love to flow through us to all God's children. We can bring God's Presence into all the circles of our lives: to our families and friends; to the streets, the subways, and the workplace; to the parish, the supermarket and the gym. Grace enables all of us: young and old, male and female, sick and well, married and single, wealthy and homeless, to be instruments of God's peace and love in our troubled world; to bring love where there is hatred, healing where there is injury, and wholeness where there are broken pieces. We are strengthened by grace; we are sanctified by the Holy Spirit to use our unique gifts, especially the experience of our own brokenness, to make the world a better place; to help bring about the

Kingdom of God here and now; to live what we pray. *Sanctification* is God's gift of transformation. It enables us to find our way back home while we help to bring about the Kingdom of God on earth.

God, the source of all goodness and love, created us. He came into our time and space to rescue us from our mistakes and redeem us by example. God sanctifies us, over and over again, with sufficient grace to transform ourselves into instruments of his love and to help bring about his Kingdom now and forever.

The Catholic doctrines of *God, Redemption,* and *Sanctification* are the pillars of my faith and the faith of the Church. They enable us to live our faith as a verb; to act on it within our relationships with God and with each other, rather than keeping it locked away inside our heads like a noun. These doctrines help us to understand who God is so that we, in turn, may gradually come to understand who God wants each of us to be.

As doctrines these are three intellectual constructs which open a channel between our minds and our souls. That channel enables God's message to reach and activate us in a manner in which our minds, locked in time and space as they are for now, can understand. God's message is that we are deeply loved; that he can't wait for us to return home; and that, while we are in the here and now of time and space, God needs us to be the hands and feet and voice of his love.

August 2004
Saint Mary's University of Minnesota

Being a Deacon

When God decided to make you and me, he did the same thing that he had done when he made every human being. He embraced each one of us like a mother would bundle up a beloved child about to go out into the cold for the very first time. And like a parent might slip a little identification note into a child's pocket, just in case he or she should get lost, God put a little tiny piece of himself inside of each of us. That little piece of God inside of you and me is our immortal soul; and life is the journey of our soul back home to its loving creator.

God sends each of us into our journey with a special plan. It is our calling in life, our vocation; it is the road that we are meant to travel on our journey back home to God. The Holy Spirit is always there to guide us on our journey; to tap us on the shoulder and point the way whenever we get a little lost; to help us discern which way to go when we reach a fork in the road; to help us get back up when we fall down.

My life journey has been very blessed. My vocation has three dimensions: I am a husband, a father, and a deacon. My wife and I were high school sweethearts. In January we will celebrate our 40th anniversary by renewing our marriage vows for the fourth time. God blessed us by sending us four children to love and nurture.

In 1984 I felt the Holy Spirit tapping me on the shoulder, inviting me to serve God and my brothers and sisters as a deacon. After eight years of discernment and formation, I received the sacrament of Holy Orders and was ordained by Cardinal McCarrick in 1992.

So, what is a deacon? First and foremost, a deacon is a servant. The archetype, the role model for all deacons is Jesus washing the feet of his disciples at the Last Supper. Through our baptism, we are all called to diaconal service to even the least of our sisters and brothers.

The book of Acts tells the story of the Apostles choosing seven people to take care of the social welfare needs of the community and to carry the gospel into the marketplaces and the trenches of society. Tradition holds that these were the first deacons. Saint Stephen was one of these seven. He was also the Church's first martyr; he was stoned to death while preaching in the city square. Perhaps the best known deacon in history is Saint Francis of Assisi.

Somewhere in the Middle Ages the Church did away with the role of deacon as a permanent state in life and made the diaconate a transitional step on the way to priesthood. But in the late 1940s, a group of priests, who had been imprisoned in a Nazi concentration camp during WWII, discerned the need to bring back the role of deacon as it was originally intended — to carry the gospel and the ministry of loving service into the prisons, the hospitals, the marketplaces and the fringes of our world. They petitioned the Pope to restore the ordained ministry of the permanent deacon.

The Second Vatican Council restored the permanent diaconate in the mid 1960s and opened it to married as well as single men. And in 1975 the Archdiocese of Newark ordained its first class of permanent deacons. Today there are approximately 300 deacons in service to our Archdiocese of Newark.

But what is it that deacons do? While you may see the deacon visibly at Mass or performing baptisms or officiating at weddings, the real thrust of the deacon's life is still social welfare — loving service to people who are disenfranchised, who live on the fringes of society; people who need someone to come along, scoop them up and bring them into the healing presence of Jesus.

Deacons have jobs and support themselves and their families. We also minister in prisons, hospitals, shelters, parishes, and offices. Being a deacon is a 24/7 vocation — we are called to loving service at every moment and in every corner of our lives.

I have been privileged to be involved in a number of ministries. Working as a team with my wife and many of our parishioners, we serve homeless people living on the streets and homeless mothers and children in shelters. I developed a youth ministry to teenagers around the martial arts, called *Holy Spirit TaeKwonDo*; led a support group for people suffering with depression and anxiety; ministered to teenagers in juvenile detention centers and adults in psychiatric hospitals.

It is a special joy for me, as a married man and as a father to perform weddings and baptize children, because I know firsthand the joys, responsibilities and challenges of marriage and parenthood.

The greatest blessing that God gave me was when I met and fell in love with my wife. The next greatest blessing was the privilege of being a father and raising our children. And without question after my wife and children, my greatest blessing was my vocation to serve the Lord as a deacon.

There is a hymn we occasionally sing at Mass that sums up why I became a deacon. The words are as follows:

> *Lord, you are my shepherd,*
> *you are my friend,*
> *I want to follow you always,*
> *just to follow my friend.*

Because the Lord is My Shepherd
© 1985, Christopher Walker.OCP

April 2007
Newark, NJ Archdiocesan Youth Retreat

Why I Am Here

Like everyone else, I was meant to be. Logically, I don't see it. There are so many, many people existing today in the present row of the matrix called, *'alive now, at this instant, snapshot, in time.'* And each column in this endless row goes back to somewhere in forever, and will go forward to somewhere in eternity.

And so many people are, have been, and will be limited in options, choices, potential. So many people have done awful things. So many, many, many: sometimes it's like thousands of ants. Across, up and down time. How could each and every one have been meant to be? How can each and every one be personally known and loved and called by name by God? How can so many have dropped by the wayside, through chance or choice, through environment or genetics?

Logically, I don't buy it; yet intuitively, I know it's true. Somewhere in the big picture it all fits together. There is free will, and at the same time there are overpowering conditions that wipe out true freedom to choose good over evil, love over hate. But God takes it all into account and makes the necessary adjustments. I'm not sure how it works, but Jesus tried to explain in the parable of the prodigal son.

God loves unconditionally to the point where someone with less capacity than God for love can never really understand. Looking through the eyes of a son or daughter of God, it really is unfair — grossly unfair. How can the bad son be loved as much as the good son. Where's the justice? How can the kidnapper, the bigot, and the torturer be embraced by God and have a seat at the same table as the saint? Where's the justice?

God's justice is not our justice. We can only see the kindergarten classroom when the tower of blocks has been knocked down, and the child who worked so hard to build it experiences the loss of 'everything.' Our vision cannot see past, present and future all existing together — that is God's vision, it is his kingdom.

So, like everyone else, I was meant to be. My choices have been skewed by circumstances beyond my control, but God adjusts. He just asks us to keep plugging along and not give up on trying to be what Jesus called us, all of us, to be — 100% selflessly in love with God and with each other.

Now the word 'God' is abstract. I intuitively know that there is a central, knowing, loving personal source of all creation. I use the word 'God' but the concept goes beyond language, beyond culture and religion. Carole King wrote a song, *Only Love is Real, Everything Else an Illusion.* Saint John preached that God is Love. So 'God' and 'Love' have the same meaning. Whether we call it 'The Force', 'The Tao', 'God', 'Nature', 'Love', it's the same essence. And whether we believe that it knows us intellectually with a mind that uses language and constructs like the human mind, or that it knows us in some other way that is beyond the limits of our comprehension – it still *knows* and *loves* each and every one of us.

I think I'm here to be what I am: a dad, a husband, a leader, a deacon. I'm here to love, and I really do love. I'm not 100% present to others like I wish I were. I have hurt others, others who depended on me. I really and truly am sorry for the people I have wounded. And yet, I think I have grown as a person, as a follower of Jesus, and that I will continue to grow, and continue to fall big time. But with the grace that has been given me, I will keep trying to love God and others with my whole heart. God adjusts.

And it is the same for everyone, I think, within the framework of their own limitations, as long as they don't give up. I want to believe that ultimately God makes things right and everyone — even the torturer, even the kidnapper, even the bigot — experiences redemption and conversion to God's love, and is made whole with God. I'm not sure, but I don't really need to be sure. That's for God to handle. I just need to keep trying my best to be who I am. I am here to love. God is love. Love is a verb, love is a noun. I am here to be in active motion; to journey towards a timeless constant, the constant that I am comfortable to label 'God'.

February 2002
Carmel Retreat House

Thank You

Thank you, Lord, for making me and sending me into your world.

Thank you for the gift of faith and for a loving heart.

Thank you for Jesus and for his presence in the Eucharist.

Thank you for the gift of meeting Wanda and journeying through life with her. She is my soul mate, my best friend, my lover and the love of my life.

Thank you for sending each one of my beloved children into my life and allowing me to help them on their journeys and to share part of those journeys with them. Danny, David, Julie and Meg are wonderful souls and have each brought much grace into my life.

Thank you for my sense of humor, for my thirst for knowledge and my desire to serve you and others.

Thank you for ministry and for martial arts and for IT which has enabled me to build a comfortable life for myself and my family.

Thank you for my mom and my dad and my Aunt Jo.

Thank you for the gift of laughter and for the great gift of lovemaking.

Thank you for the joy of gathering at table with my family and the love that is present.

Thank you, Lord, for everything.

Movies, Songs and Books Referenced

Blakney, Raymond Bernard. <u>Meister Eckhart: A Modern Translation</u>. New York: Harper Torchbooks. 1941.

Collins, Mary, O.S.B. <u>Spirituality Today</u>. March 1982.

Crystal, Billy. *City Slickers*. Columbia TriStar. 1991.

Endo, Shusaku. <u>The Final Martyrs</u>. New York: New Directions. 1959.

Godspell. Columbia Pictures. 1973.

Jackson, Michael. "We Are The World." New York: Sony ATV. 1987.

Keitel, Harvey. *The Bad Lieutenant.* Aries Films. 1992.

King, Carole. "Only Love Is Real." By Carole King. <u>Thoroughbred</u>. Capitol. 1976.

McDonnell, Kilian, O.S.B. <u>The Other Hand of God: The Holy Spirit as the Universal Touch and Goal</u>. Minnesota: Liturgical Press. 2003.

Menken, Alan and Rice, Tim. "A Whole New World." *Aladdin.* Disney Films. 1992.

Scorsese, Martin. *The Last Temptation of Christ.* Universal Picture. 1988.

Walker, Christopher. "Because the Lord Is My Shepherd." By Christopher Walker. OCP Publications. 1985.

Wilkes, Paul. <u>7 Secrets of Successful Catholics</u>. New Jersey: Paulist Press. 1998.

Windley-Daoust, Susan, Ph.D. <u>The Redeemed Image of God: Embodied Relations to the Unknown Divine</u>. Maryland: University Press of America, 2002.

7722218R0

Made in the USA
Charleston, SC
03 April 2011